GOD
IS A
WARRIOR

Books in This Series

STUDIES IN
OLD TESTAMENT BIBLICAL THEOLOGY

GOD IS A WARRIOR

TREMPER LONGMAN III & DANIEL G. REID

ZondervanPublishingHouse

Grand Rapids, Michigan

A Division of HarperCollinsPublishers

God Is a Warrior
Copyright © 1995 by Tremper Longman III and Daniel G. Reid

Requests for information should be addressed to:
  Zondervan Publishing House
  Grand Rapids, MI 49530

Library of Congress Cataloging-in-Publication Data

Longman, Tremper.
    God is a warrior / by Tremper Longman III and Daniel G. Reid.
      p. cm.
    Includes bibliographical references and index.
    ISBN: 0-310-49461-3 (softcover)
    1. War–Biblical teaching. 2. Military history in the Bible. 3. Bible–Criticism,
Interpretation, etc. I. Reid, Daniel G., 1949–
BS680.W2L66 1994
220.6'4-dc 20   94-40876
                                                                      CIP

Edited by Verlyn D. Verbrugge

Printed in the United States of America

    96 97 98 99 00 / ❖ DH / 10 9 8 7 6 5 4 3 2

◆ Contents ◆

Contents

◆ Preface to Series ◆

The editors are pleased to announce the "Studies in Old Testament Biblical Theology" series, with the hope that it contributes to the field of Old Testament theology and stimulates further discussion. If Old Testament theology is the queen of Old Testament studies, she is a rather neglected queen. To write in the area of Old Testament theology is a daunting proposition, one that leads many to hesitate taking on the task. After all, Old Testament theology presupposes an understanding of all the books of the Old Testament and, at least as conceived in the present project, an insight into its connection with the New Testament.

Another reason why theology has been neglected in recent years is simply a lack of confidence that the Old Testament can be summarized in one or even a number of volumes. Is there a center, a central concept, under which the entire Old Testament may be subsumed? Many doubt it. Thus, while a number of articles, monographs, and commentaries address the theology of a source, a chapter, or even a book, few studies address the Old Testament as a whole.

The editors of this series also believe it is impossible to present the entirety of the Old Testament message under a single rubric. Even as important a concept as the covenant fails to incorporate all aspects of the Old Testament (note especially wisdom literature). Thus, this series will present separate volumes, each devoted to a different theme, issue, or perspective of biblical theology, and will show its importance for the Old Testament and for the entire Christian canon.

One last word needs to be said about theological approach. Gone are the days when scholars, especially those who work in a filed as ideologically sensitive as theology, can claim neutrality by hiding behind some kind of scientific methodology. It is, therefore, important to announce the approach taken in this series. Those who know the editors, authors, and publisher will not be surprised to learn that an evangelical approach is taken throughout this series. At the same time, however, we believe that those who do not share this starting point may still benefit and learn from these studies.

The general editors of this series, Willem A. VanGemeren and Tremper Longman III, wish to thank the academic publishing department of Zondervan, particularly Stan Gundry and Verlyn Verbrugge, who will be working most closely with the series.

Willem A. VanGemeren
Professor of Old Testament and Semitic Languages
Trinity Evangelical Divinity School

◆ Preface ◆

Fifteen years ago I gave my first public scholarly lecture at the Evangelical Theological Society meeting in Toronto. The subject was "The Divine Warrior: The New Testament Use of an Old Testament Motif." It is testimony to my prematurely failing memory that I cannot remember what first caught my interest in this theme, but I do recall the wonder that I felt that after so many years of reading the Bible I had never before noticed how pervasive the theme of God's battles was.

I became so enraptured by the theme that it was soon a standing joke around Westminster Theological Seminary that I lectured on it at a drop of a hat. I have since moved on to a number of other topics that have also engaged my professional and personal attention, but have continued to be deeply affected in my thinking and life by the biblical portrait of Yahweh as a warrior. It is with a great deal of satisfaction that Dan and I have been able to work on this project together and bring it to publication.

It was a pleasure to work with Dan Reid on this project. The lecture I delivered at the ETS meeting in Toronto was published in 1982, the same year that Dan finished his doctoral dissertation on the same subject. Our mutual interest soon found us communicating with each other, and the joint project was soon born. It has been enjoyable and instructive. I am happy that other projects in process will keep us in communication.

I would like to thank Zondervan Publishing House for their willingness to publish this work and, in particular, Stan Gundry, Ed Van der Maas, Len Goss (now at Crossway), and Verlyn Verbrugge.

Most of all I thank my wife, Alice, and my three sons, Tremper IV, Timothy, and Andrew, for their support.

Tremper Longman III

◆ 9 ◆

◆ Preface ◆

This book started as a paper on Isaiah 13 and led to the clarification of my dissertation topic at Fuller Theological Seminary, "The Christus Victor Motif in Pauline Theology," supervised by Ralph P. Martin and John D. W. Watts. I am grateful to them for their proddings, correction, and encouragement.

In 1982 I discovered a fellow traveler in Tremper Longman, whose article on "The Divine Warrior: The New Testament Use of an Old Testament Motif" captured my attention. Two years of teaching at Asian Theological Seminary, Manila, Philippines, provided the opportunity to consider the theme in a Third World setting of political and spiritual oppression. I learned much from the students there.

In 1986 Tremper Longman and I met at the SBL and discussed our mutual interest in writing a book on the divine warrior. The present series provided a venue for exploring our mutual interest. Tremper has helped crystallize my own perspective on the divine warrior in the Old Testament and against the ancient Near Eastern background. Renewed opportunities to teach biblical studies at Fuller Seminary's extension in Seattle also helped clarify some issues. I am indebted to those students who have asked questions or added their insights. Several years of editorial work on the *Dictionary of Jesus and the Gospels* and the *Dictionary of Paul and his Letters* have put me in quiet conversation with a range of scholars too numerous to mention, though Graham Twelftree and Rikki Watts are especially due for thanks for providing me with their scholarly expertise.

Preeminent in patience with this preoccupation and in allowing me the time to write are my wife Cyndy, my daughter Lindsey, and my son Colin. I give them my wholehearted thanks.

Daniel Reid

◆ Abbreviations ◆

AB	The Anchor Bible
AnBib	Analecta Biblica
ANET	J. B. Prichard (ed), *Ancient Near Eastern Texts*
ASOR	American Scholars of Oriental Research
BAG	Bauer, Arndt, Gingrich, *Greek-English Lexicon of the New Testament*
BASOR	*Bulletin of the American Schools of Oriental Research*
Bib	*Biblica*
BibOr	Biblica et orientalia
BJRL	*Bulletin of the John Rylands Library of Manchester*
BJS	Brown Judaic Studies
CBQ	*Catholic Biblical Quarterly*
CBQMS	*Catholic Biblical Quarterly* (Monograph Series)
CGTC	Cambridge Greek Testament Commentary
CTA	A. Herdner, *Corpus des tablettes en cunéiformes alphabétiques*
DJG	*Dictionary of Jesus and the Gospels*
DPL	*Dictionary of Paul and His Letters*
EQ	*Evangelical Quarterly*
ExpT	*Expository Times*
Grace Th J	*Grace Theological Journal*
HDR	Harvard Dissertations in Religion
Herm.	Hermeneia
HSM	Harvard Semitic Monographs
HTR	*Harvard Theological Revue*
HUCA	*Hebrew Union College Annual*
IDB Sup	*Interpreter's Dictionary of the Bible* (Supplement)
Int	*Interpretation: A Journal of Bible and Theology*
JAOS	*Journal of the American Oriental Society*
JBL	*Journal of Biblical Literature*
JETS	*Journal of the Evangelical Theological Society*
JSNT	*Journal for the Study of the New Testament*
JSNTSup	*Journal for the Study of the New Testament* (Supplement Series)
JSS	*Journal of Semitic Studies*
NCB	New Century Bible
NICNT	The New International Commentary on the New Testament
NIDNTT	*New International Dictionary of New Testament Theology*
NovT	*Novum Testamentum*

NTS	*New Testament Studies*
OTL	Old Testament Library
Rev. Q	*Revue de Qumran*
RTJ	*Reformed Theological Journal*
SBLDS	Society of Biblical Literature Dissertation Series
SBT	Studies in Biblical Theology
Semeia	*Semeia: An Experimental Journal for Biblical Criticism*
SJT	*Scottish Journal of Theology*
SNTSMS	Society for New Testament Studies Monograph Series
TDNT	Kittel: *Theological Dictionary of the New Testament*
THWAT	*Theologisches Handwörterbuch zum alten Testament*
TNTC	The Tyndale New Testament Commentaries
TOTC	Tyndale Old Testament Commentaries
VT	*Vetus Testamentum*
VTS	*Vetus Testamentum* (Supplements)
WBC	Word Biblical Commentary
WTJ	*Westminster Theological Journal*
WUNT	Wissenschaftliche Untersuchungen zum neuen Testament
ZAW	*Zeitschrift für die alttestamentliche Wissenschaft*
ZNW	*Zeitschrift für die neutestamentliche Wissenschaft*

◆ 1 ◆

The Divine Warrior
as a Central Biblical Motif

On the surface, the Bible is a diverse collection of writings, a veritable anthology of different literary works.[1] The reader encounters a wide variety of genres produced over a long span of time by countless authors. In the midst of diversity, however, the careful reader is drawn into the organic unity of the Bible. Though it is often difficult to explain, the Bible's message coheres on a profound level. This message cuts across time and genres, so that not only is the Bible composed of many different stories, we may also say that it tells a single story.

How is this unity to be described? How can it be presented without losing sight of the proper diversity of the Bible? At least in part, the answer to these questions is found in the major themes of the Bible. The present study focuses on one of the most pervasive of all biblical themes: the divine warrior.

---

[1]A popular introduction to the different literary types in the Bible is found in John H. Balchin, David H. Field, and Tremper Longman III, *The Complete Bible Study Tool Kit* (Downers Grove, Ill.: InterVarsity Press, 1991).

THE TASK OF BIBLICAL THEOLOGY

The discovery of the unity of biblical revelation is the concern of biblical theology. As John Murray[2] pointed out, biblical theology finds its place between exegesis and systematic theology. The former is the interpretation of individual texts and informs biblical theology that seeks to describe the message of the Bible as a whole. The latter, systematic theology, like biblical theology, deals with the whole message of the Bible but answers modern questions using modern categories. Biblical theology, on the other hand, describes phenomena within the Bible using biblical categories.

There are many approaches to biblical theology, but they may be divided into two types: those that posit a single center to biblical revelation, and those that allow for many different avenues of approach. Increasingly, biblical scholars opt for the latter since the argument for a single center founders on the inability to describe all of biblical revelation. In other words, the message of the Bible is so rich that its unity cannot be reduced to a single category, unless it becomes so broad as to be useless. In Reformed circles, for instance, covenant is widely accepted as the center of biblical theology.[3] Indeed, it is an extremely important biblical theme. It is impossible, however, to subsume all of biblical revelation under its rubric. For instance, Old Testament wisdom literature does not explicitly interact with covenant theology, so that attempts to describe wisdom literature in a covenant theology[4] must struggle to the point of

---

[2]J. Murray, "Systematic Theology: Second Article," *WTJ* 26 (1963): 33–46.

[3]See most notably, O. P. Robertson, *The Christ of the Covenants* (Phillipsburg, N.J.: Presbyterian and Reformed, 1980). Contemporary Reformed interest in the covenant is likely motivated in large part by the important organizing role that the covenant concept plays in the "Westminster Confession of Faith."

[4]M. G. Kline, *Structure of Biblical Authority* (Grand Rapids: Eerdmans, 1972), argues that wisdom's place in the covenant is illuminated by the connection between biblical covenants and ancient Near Eastern treaties. Law

straining the evidence. As a matter of fact, wisdom literature, since it is different in character from most biblical revelation, has been a major obstacle to attempts to describe the center of biblical theology.

A multiperspectival approach[5] to biblical theology is more in keeping with the rich and subtle nature of biblical revelation. The question that biblical theology asks is: What is the message of the Bible? The answer is that the Bible is about Yahweh.[6] It is his self-revelation. The Bible, however, is not about Yahweh in the abstract; it is about God in relation to humankind. Furthermore, this relationship is not so much described as it is narrated. There is a historical dimension to biblical revelation. Thus, a proper biblical theology must take into account the subject matter of the Bible, the divine-human relationship, and the fact that the Bible's message is told through time.

A multiperspectival approach to biblical theology is the natural consequence of this. After all, God's relationship with his people is presented by means of a variety of metaphors that emphasize different aspects of that relationship. No one metaphor is capable of capturing the richness of God's nature or the wonder of his relationship with his creatures. God's compassion and love for his creatures lie behind the image of the mother-child relationship (Ps 131) as well as the marriage metaphor (SS). His ability to guide his people is suggested by the shepherd-sheep image (Ps 23). Yahweh's wisdom is displayed in the figure of Lady Wisdom (Pr 8–9). God's power and authority over his people are communicated through a wide variety of images, including that of king (the covenant-

---

plays an important role in the treaty, as it does in covenant texts like the book of Deuteronomy and Exodus 19–20. He attempts to situate wisdom in the picture by noting its connection with law by virtue of its imperatival nature.

[5]The most persuasive argument in favor of a multiperspectival approach is found in V. S. Poythress, *Symphonic Theology* (Grand Rapids: Zondervan, 1987).

[6]S. L. Terrien, *The Elusive Presence: Toward a New Biblical Theology* (New York: Harper & Row, 1978).

treaty image finds its place here) and the concern of the present book—God as divine warrior.

The most fruitful biblical-theological studies are those that focus on one of these important metaphors of relationship and follow it from the beginning of biblical revelation to its end, from Genesis to Revelation. A number of years ago, G. Vos,[7] the father of modern evangelical biblical theology,[8] showed how divine revelation was a reflex to the history of redemption. Thus, as God's redemptive plan progressed through the ages, so the history of revelation unfolded.[9]

THE DIVINE WARRIOR
AND BIBLICAL THEOLOGY

One important and pervasive metaphor of relationship is the picture of God as a warrior, commonly referred to in secondary literature as the divine-warrior theme. It is our purpose to study the divine-warrior theme through the history of redemption, showing how the concept developed as revelation unfolded. The results are an illuminating study in the continuity and discontinuity between the different epochs of divine revelation, most notably between the Old and New Testa-

[7]See in particular G. Vos, *Biblical Theology* (Grand Rapids: Eerdmans, 1948), a book that is still used as a textbook in a number of Reformed seminaries.

[8]To be differentiated from the biblical theology of critical scholarship of the 1950s whose death was proclaimed in the 1960s and 1970s. See B. S. Childs, *Biblical Theology in Crisis* (Philadelphia: Westminster, 1970). He presents a canonical approach to the subject in *Old Testament Theology in a Canonical Context* (Philadelphia: Fortress, 1986) and, more recently, *Biblical Theology of the Old and New Testaments* (Minneapolis: Augsburg Fortress, 1992).

[9]Indeed, it is interesting to note how God announces through revelation that a great redemptive act will occur in the future. He then performs that act. Finally, he interprets the act through revelation. Of course, the greatest such redemptive act is the Cross, which was revealed as a future event in the Old Testament and then described and interpreted in the Gospels and letters of the New Testament.

ments. We may conceive of the development of the theme following a roughly chronological scheme by describing the process as taking place in five stages. The first stage is God's appearance as a warrior who fights on behalf of his people Israel against their flesh-and-blood enemies. The second stage overlaps with the first, yet culminates Israel's independent political history as God fights in judgment against Israel itself. The Old Testament period ends during the third stage as Israel's prophets look to the future and proclaim the advent of a powerful divine warrior. While many studies of the divine warrior are restricted to the Old Testament, we will show its development into the New Testament. The Gospels and letters reflect on the fourth stage, Christ's earthly ministry as the work of a conqueror, though they also look forward to the next stage. The fifth and final stage is anticipated by the church as it awaits the return of the divine warrior who will judge the spiritual and human enemies of God. These five stages may be graphically represented in the following way:

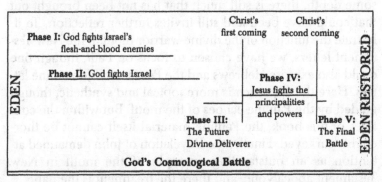

The pervasiveness of the theme of the divine warrior in the Old Testament, as well as the length and complexity of that portion of the canon, suggests that a synthetic approach to the Old Testament material is more manageable. It is hoped that this approach will allow the reader to grasp more readily the main features of the motif and their significance.

In Part 1, which covers the Old Testament, we will devote several chapters to stage one (Israel's deliverance, chap. 2), stage two (Israel's judgment, chap. 3), and stage three (Israel's hope, chap. 4). In addition, there is in the Bible a battle that stands behind this fivefold development. It interacts with these five stages in that they are earthly manifestations of this heavenly reality. This battle is God's war with the forces of chaos on the cosmic level, which will be described in chapter 5. The themes of holy war and divine warrior are connected with similar yet distinct ideas in the broader ancient Near East. The Near Eastern background will be described in the last chapter of Part 1.

Turning to the New Testament, we find that the use of the divine-warrior motif in the Gospels is, for the most part, more subtly woven into the texture of the narrative. Surprisingly few commentators have recognized the echoes of the motif as it runs through the text of the Gospels. Thus, a more textual approach has been taken. And while the theme is explored at some depth, there is still much that has not been brought out that could have been and still invites further reflection. To illustrate the function of the divine-warrior motif in the New Testament letters, we have chosen to focus on Paul, though one could also explore Hebrews and the Petrine and Johannine letters. Here the approach is more topical and synthetic, though guided by the Pauline echoes of the motif. But within the confines of this book, the Pauline material itself cannot be thoroughly surveyed. Finally, the Revelation of John demanded attention as an outstanding example of the motif in New Testament apocalyptic, and there the treatment is thematic.

Thus, Part 2 will cover the New Testament on the basis of a threefold distinction between Gospel, letter, and apocalypse. The treatment of stages four and five in the progress of divine revelation appears in a broken pattern. Chapters 7 and 8 survey the Synoptic Gospels (i.e., omitting John), particularly focusing on Mark. Much of these two chapters is devoted to what we have called stage four, Jesus' war against Satan and the spiritual powers during his earthly ministry, and culminating in the Cross. An important part of chapter 8, however, deals with the return of the divine warrior, or stage five.[10]

Chapters 9 and 10 survey the Pauline letters. Chapter 9, in particular, examines Paul's use of divine-warrior imagery in regard to the crucifixion and resurrection (stage four), while chapter 10 probes the theme both in relationship to the church's role in the world and Paul's understanding of the future.[11] Chapter 11 concludes our study with Revelation, and in keeping with the content of that book, exclusively addresses stage five.

PREVIOUS RESEARCH

It has long been recognized that God appeared to his ancient people as a warrior. John Calvin, in his commentary on Exodus 15:3, describes God as "armed in military attire, to contend with all of the forces of his foes."[12] The discussion of this biblical theme, however, has taken concrete focus within the past century.

Ben Ollenburger has provided an English translation of von Rad's *Holy War in Ancient Israel,* a pivotal book on the subject to be described below; he prefaced his work with a description of modern treatments of the holy war theme in ancient Israel.[13] This study is insightful and overlaps with research on the divine-warrior theme. We have, accordingly, drawn much from his study and present it here primarily for

---

[10]Most notably the section entitled "The Cloud Rider Rides Again," pages 124–26.

[11]Paul's treatment of stage five may be found in the section entitled "The Future Triumph: Day of the Lord" on pp. 171–79.

[12]J. Calvin, *Commentaries on the Four Last Books of Moses,* vol. 1, trans. C. W. Bingham (Grand Rapids: Baker, 1981).

[13]In G. von Rad, *Holy War in Ancient Israel* (1958: reprint, Grand Rapids: Eerdmans, 1991), 1–33.

the convenience of the reader. New topics, however, are treated in this brief survey that are omitted from his, and he gives fuller accounts than we do of the work of some scholars.

Perhaps the most important biblical insights into holy war and the divine-warrior themes before von Rad were those of Wellhausen,[14] Schwally,[15] and Fredriksson.[16] Otto Weber, the eminent sociologist, also contributed much toward the understanding of the Old Testament's teaching on the subject.[17]

Wellhausen, who is at the foundation of so many contemporary issues of biblical scholarship, expressed his understanding of the religious nature of warfare in ancient Israel. War was worship for Israel. But even further he noted the warlike nature of Israel's religion. Israel was in conflict with her neighbors, particularly in the area of religion, and this frequently led to armed conflict.

Frederick Schwally has the distinction of being the first in the modern period to present a study devoted to holy war in ancient Israel. He did his work at the turn of the century. Like Wellhausen, Schwally realized that warfare was at the center of Israel's national and theological existence. He drew close connections between Israel's conduct of warfare on the one hand, and its worship and political federation (the covenant) on the other. As Ollenburger has pointed out, *holy war* is a term that originates with Schwally. It does not appear in the Old Testament itself, but it is legitimately applied to its teaching.

Weber continued this line of thinking. He, like his precursors, argued that war was a religious phenomenon in Israel. He saw a close connection between formal worship institutions, warfare, and covenant. God was Israel's sovereign Lord

---

[14]J. Wellhausen, *Prolegomena to the History of Ancient Israel* (1885; reprint, Atlanta: Scholars, 1994).

[15]F. Schwally, *Der heilige Krieg im alten Israel* (Leipzig: Dietrich, 1901).

[16]H. Fredriksson, *Jahwe als Krieger: Studien zum alttestamentlichen Gottesbild* (Lund: Gleerup, 1945).

[17]O. Weber, *Ancient Judaism* (1917–1919; reprint; Glencoe, Ill.: Free Press, 1952).

who promised to protect them. Weber did his work on this subject in a volume published between 1917 and 1919, and, as a sociologist, his writings exerted a wide influence.

Fredriksson's contribution has to do with the specific object of his study, the divine warrior. While most scholars up to this point examined holy war, Fredriksson described the image of the divine warrior. In this way, he is a direct precursor to the present work.

Wellhausen, Schwally, Fredriksson, and Weber preceded von Rad in an analysis of holy war and the divine-warrior theme, but von Rad is nonetheless a kind of watershed figure in the study of this institution or motif. The significance of his contribution certainly has to do with his stature within twentieth-century Old Testament scholarship, but it also results from the clarity of his writing and his ability to integrate his study of holy war into the broader issues facing biblical studies in his day. Ollenburger has done an admirable job showing how von Rad situated the study of holy war into his broader concerns, especially the study of form criticism, the Solomonic enlightenment, and Deuteronomy.[18]

Von Rad founded his study on a close reading of certain set terms associated with the waging of war. These terms cover the period of time from the blast of the trumpet, which mustered the army, to the final command to the army to return to their tribal homeland. This study led von Rad to the following statement that is foundational to his conclusions, at the end of which he quotes Wellhausen:

> Thus, we can indeed consider holy war as an eminently cultic understanding—that is, prescribed and sanctioned by fixed, traditional, sacred rites and observances. "The armed camp, the cradle of the nation, was also its most ancient holy of holies. There was Israel and there was Yahweh."[19]

---

[18]Ollenburger in von Rad, *Holy War*, 13–22.

[19]von Rad, *Holy War*, 51, quoting J. Wellhausen, *Israelitische und judische Geschichte* (Berlin: de Gruyter, 1927), 26.

When von Rad studied the historical reality of this cultic institution, however, he arrived at predominantly negative conclusions (his chap. 2). He believed that the narratives that describe holy war are written from an ideologically distorted perspective to serve the theological purposes of a later era (for instance, the Deuteronomist). This conclusion is based at least partly on von Rad's conviction that the idea of holy war was that of the entire group of tribes joining in battle. Critically speaking, the picture of the early wars of Israel as the work of "all Israel" could only be a later retrojection of this ideal on Israel's past. He thus concludes: "We deal here with a cultic institution which historically never became fully manifest in its essential and intended form."[20]

In his third chapter, von Rad explains that even the accounts of Israel's early holy wars are written from a post-Davidic perspective. This Solomonic time period had no experience of holy war, since David had set up a secularist military organization that contradicted the concept of a militia made up of free farmers who fought only when called on by God. To use distinctively von Radian language, the accounts of holy war are separated from the original events by the Solomonic enlightenment, which no longer saw all of life as sacral experience. Holy war had become a theme in a theological narrative of the past. This new perspective is seen in the cooperation that takes place between Yahweh and Israel, the new element being the emphasis on God alone bringing the victory.

Next, von Rad shows how the prophets appropriate the old patriarchal, or tribal, tradition of holy war, especially when the monarchy abandons it. He explicates a number of examples, but he is especially insightful in his discussion of Isaiah's use of the concept.[21] The connection between kingship and the prophets in relationship to the motif of holy war is an important one that is explored in chapter three of the present book.

---

[20]von Rad, *Holy War,* 69.
[21]Ibid., 101–8.

Von Rad's penultimate chapter focuses on the book of Deuteronomy. He highlights the book's importance in the development of the concept of holy war by saying, "From Deuteronomy therefore came that war ideology which through the Deuteronomistic editing of many historic books—virtually the entire Old Testament—contributed that additional element of militant spirit. . . ."[22] He believes that Deuteronomy represents a powerful resurgence of the ancient holy war tradition that occurred during the reign of Josiah. In von Rad's concept, however, Deuteronomy is a late development through whose veneer the earlier patriarchal traditions are only dimly seen.

The institution of holy war comes to a complete end with the death of Josiah. Von Rad, however, notes its literary afterlife in such post-Deuteronomic writings as 2 Chronicles 20 and the Psalms.

As mentioned, von Rad's research on holy war garnered widespread acceptance and stimulated yet further work. Nevertheless, it was not long before scholars began chipping away at his hypothesis. Smend,[23] for instance, attacked his concept of the connection between warfare and amphictyony, or tribal league, of the period of the judges. Weippert[24] elucidated Assyrian parallels that destroyed his idea of Israelite uniqueness or any idea of an ancient Near Eastern distinction between religious and profane warfare. All of this criticism has led Gottwald to say in the context of an excellent summarizing essay: "The view articulated by von Rad, that holy war referred to a homogeneous and distinctive institution and cultic matrix in Israel, is now under question."[25]

Since the 1960s Harvard University has been the seedbed for much study of the divine-warrior theme. This focus has its

---

[22]Ibid., 116.

[23]R. Smend, *Yahweh War and Tribal Confederation* (Nashville: Abingdon, 1970).

[24]M. Weippert, "'Heiligerkrieg' in Israel und Assyrian," *ZAW* 84 (1972): 460–93.

[25]N. K. Gottwald, "Holy War," *IDBS* (1976): 942.

source in the writings of F. M. Cross, one of a number of W. F. Albright's students who have dominated university posts in Old Testament from the 1960s through the late 1980s. Cross's most significant work on the divine-warrior theme may be found in his *Canaanite Myth and Hebrew Epic*.[26] The book is composed of a series of individual essays that are prolegomena to a new history of Israel's religion. When he writes of the divine-warrior theme, he concentrates on early poetry and its description of the cosmological war of Yahweh. This emphasis was expanded by his student P. D. Miller, Jr.[27] Others of his students who also contributed to the discussion in major and minor works include D. Christensen[28] and D. Stuart.[29] P. D. Hanson[30] and W. R. Millar[31] utilized the theme in their works on apocalyptic.

Holy war and divine warrior have received major attention from pacifist Mennonite scholars. Eller[32] and Yoder[33] are notable examples, but perhaps it is fair to say that Lind offers the most substantial contribution with his book *Yahweh Is a Warrior*.[34] In his work Lind argues that the early records of holy war are historically based and show that God, not hu-

---

[26]F. M. Cross, *Canaanite Myth and Hebrew Epic* (Cambridge: Harvard University Press, 1973).

[27]P. D. Miller, Jr., "Fire in the Mythology of Canaan and Israel," *CBQ* 27 (1965): 256–61.

[28]D. L. Christensen, *Transformations of the War Oracle*, HDR (Missoula, Mont.: Scholars, 1975).

[29]D. Stuart, "The Sovereign's Day of Conquest," *BASOR* 221 (1976): 159–64.

[30]P. D. Hanson, *The Dawn of Apocalyptic* (Philadelphia: Fortress, 1975).

[31]W. R. Millar, *Isaiah 24–27 and the Origin of Apocalyptic*, HSM, vol. 11 (Missoula, Mont.: Scholars, 1976).

[32]V. Eller, *War and Peace from Genesis to Revelation* (Scottdale, Pa.: Herald, 1981).

[33]J. H. Yoder, *The Original Revolution: Essays on Christian Pacifism* (Scottdale, Pa.: Herald, 1977) and "'To Your Tents, O Israel': The Legacy of Israel's Experience with Holy War," in *Studies in Religion/Sciences religieuses* 18 (1989): 345–62.

[34]M. C. Lind, *Yahweh Is a Warrior* (Scottdale, Pa.: Herald, 1980).

mans, is the one who wins victories. He also notes that both early and late traditions highlight God's fighting activity and downplay human involvement. God's miraculous intervention provides the victory, an intervention that is often modelled after the deliverance at the Red Sea. God's warring activity is intimately connected with his kingship.

The appeal of holy war and divine warrior to pacifist circles is not difficult to understand. As Lind points out, warfare is a divine activity in the Old Testament that is mediated not by a "warrior" but by a Moses-like "prophet." Thus, holy war is a divine, not a human prerogative.

Studies of holy war and the divine warrior increased through the 1980s and into the 1990s. In many cases, the authors provide short specialized studies that continue in the traditions of those who have preceded them (for instance, the studies by Conrad,[35] Greenspoon,[36] and Kloos[37]). Indeed, we note no major transitions in this period except the increasing sensitivity to the presence of these themes in the New Testament.[38] Two major emphases in the 1980s and 1990s are research into the ancient Near Eastern background to the biblical institution or theme[39] and further explorations of God's

---

[35]E. W. Conrad, *Fear Not Warrior: A Study of the 'al tira' Pericopes in the Hebrew Scriptures,* BJS, vol. 75 (Chico, Calif.: Scholars, 1985).

[36]L. J. Greenspoon, "The Origin of the Idea of Resurrection," in *Traditions in Transformation,* ed. B. Halperin and J. D. Levenson (Winona Lake, Ind.: Eisenbrauns, 1981), 247–321.

[37]C. Kloos, *Yhwh's Combat with the Sea: A Canaanite Tradition in the Religion of Ancient Israel* (Leiden: Brill, 1986) and "The Flood on Speaking Terms with God," *ZAW* 94 (1982): 639–42.

[38]T. Longman III, "The Divine Warrior: The New Testament Use of an Old Testament Motif," *WTJ* 44 (1982): 290–307; D. Reid, "The Christus Victor Motif in Paul's Theology" (Ph.D. diss., Fuller Theological Seminary, 1982); F. R. McCurley, *Ancient Myths and Biblical Faith: Scriptural Transformations* (Philadelphia: Fortress, 1983); R. E. Watts, "The Influence of the Isaianic New Exodus on the Gospel of Mark" (Ph.D. diss., The University of Cambridge, 1990).

[39]S.-M. Kang, *Divine War in the Old Testament and in the Ancient Near East* (New York: de Gruyter, 1989); M. Weinfeld, "*kabod,*" *THWAT* 4:23–40.

conflict with the forces of cosmic chaos.[40] It is also characteristic of recent trends in biblical hermeneutic that the divine-warrior theme has been studied from the perspective of late twentieth-century feminism.[41]

THE SCOPE AND
CONTRIBUTION OF THE STUDY

In the light of the impressive history of research especially since von Rad, it is appropriate to raise the question of the contribution of the present volume. In the first place, our study concentrates on the image of God as divine warrior, not the institution of holy war per se. Of course, the image occurs in close connection with the institution; thus we will describe holy war and set our understanding of the divine warrior in its context.

In the second place, we approach the Bible as an organic whole. For the purpose of this volume, we do not prejudge the process of composition of biblical books nor deny different theological tendencies within the Old Testament, but in the final analysis we treat the Old Testament, even the Bible as a whole, as a single writing that presents an internally consistent message, including an internally consistent, yet unfolding picture of God as a warrior. While this approach could be justified by an appeal to recent canon theology[42] or literary ap-

---

[40]J. Day, *God's Conflict with the Dragon and the Sea* (Cambridge: Cambridge University Press, 1975); Kloos, *Yhwh's Combat*; M. K. Wakeman, *God's Battle with the Monster. A Study in Biblical Imagery* (Leiden: Brill, 1973).

[41]C. P. Christ, "Feminist Liberation Theology and Yahweh as Holy Warrior: An Analysis of Symbol," in *Women's Spirit Bonding*, ed. J. Kalven and M. I. Buckley (New York: Pilgrim, 1984), 202–12.

[42]For one of his most notable statements and applications of his canonical theology, see B. S. Childs, *Introduction to the Old Testament as Scripture* (Philadelphia: Fortress, 1979).

proaches,[43] for us the basic ground is a theological one based on the self-attestation of Scripture that leads us to an evangelical hermeneutic.[44] The organic wholeness of the Bible allows the kind of study advocated by Vos and VanGemeren[45] and followed here. Nonetheless, we believe that those of our readers who do not hold these theological convictions can benefit from our study on literary grounds, especially intertextuality.[46]

The most notable implication of such a methodological approach is the relationship between the image of God as divine warrior in the Old Testament and the presentation of Jesus Christ as warrior in the New. Both of us[47] independently produced preliminary studies of the New Testament motif in 1982. Since that time, a handful of other scholars have alluded to the theme,[48] but the present study is the first full-scale exposition of the connection.

We do not intend to discuss or cite every passage that is relevant to the image of the divine warrior. Such a study is inconceivable, given the incredible pervasiveness of the theme. It is our hope to lay bare the outline of the biblical-theological development of the theme and in this way provide a grid for the reader to understand other passages and texts.

---

[43]J. Barton, *Reading the Old Testament* (Philadelphia: Westminster, 1984); T. Longman, *Literary Approaches to Biblical Interpretation* (Grand Rapids: Zondervan, 1987).

[44]R. B. Gaffin, "The New Testament as Canon," in *Inerrancy and Hermeneutic* (Grand Rapids: Baker, 1988), 165–83.

[45]Vos, *Biblical Theology*; W. VanGemeren, *The Progress of Redemption: The Story of Salvation from Creation to the New Jerusalem* (Grand Rapids: Zondervan, 1988).

[46]J. Kristeva, *Semiotiké: Recherches pour une sémanalyse* (Paris: Seuil, 1969).

[47]Longman, "The Divine Warrior Motif"; Reid, "The Christus Victor Motif in Paul's Theology."

[48]McCurley, *Ancient Myths and Biblical Faith*; Watts, "The Influence of the Isaianic New Exodus on the Gospel of Mark."

PART 1

The Old Testament

◆ 2 ◆

God Is a Warrior:
The Wars of Faithful Israel

According to the book of Exodus, Israel experienced the presence of Yahweh as a warrior early in its national existence.[1] As Israel fled from Egyptian bondage, God revealed himself as the protector and deliverer of his people. The Egyptian army had trapped the weaponless Israelites at the shore of the Red Sea. As they approached, however, the sea opened, allowing them to cross safely. Afterward, it closed on the Egyptians as they attempted to follow their prey. The Israelites knew that this unprecedented deliverance was no freak of nature and testified to it as an act of God in the Song of Moses:

> I will sing to the LORD,
>   for he is highly exalted.
> The horse and its rider
>   he has hurled into the sea.
> The LORD is my strength and my song;
>   he has become my salvation.
> He is my God, and I will praise him,
>   my father's God, and I will exalt him.
> The LORD is a warrior;
>   the LORD is his name. (Ex 15:1–3)

---

[1]Exodus 15 is considered to be among the earliest parts of the Old Testament even by those who deny the biblical tradition of Mosaic origins. See F. M. Cross, "The Song of the Sea and Canaanite Myth," in *Canaanite Myth and Hebrew Epic* (Cambridge: Harvard University Press, 1973), 112–44 and D. N. Freedman, *Pottery, Poetry, and Prophecy* (Winona Lake, Ind.: Eisenbrauns, 1980), 176–78.

This poem represents the first explicit statement of the warlike nature of God. As we will see in the following study, this theme of God as a warrior became a recurrent refrain in the Old Testament. The Exodus event itself became an important archetype in the biblical tradition, a means of telling and retelling God's acts of deliverance. God often dramatically revealed himself to the Israelites as the one who saved them from physical harm. He fought against their enemies.

The theme of the divine warrior, however, has a background in the concept of holy war. While pursuing the theme of God as a warrior, we will describe the institution of holy war in the Old Testament.

HOLY WAR IN ANCIENT ISRAEL

In ancient Israel, all of life was religious, all of life was related to God. Warfare was no exception. Indeed, the biblical text is a witness to Israel's understanding of God's pervasive role in its warfare. Two types of text are especially relevant to a study of holy war in the Hebrew Bible: law and historical narrative. In particular, Deuteronomy 7 and 20 set forth the legal parameters for the waging of war. In addition, innumerable historical narratives illuminate the practice and theory of holy war. While we will cite prophecy and psalms in our description, what follows is primarily a synthesis of legal and historical materials. Prophecy will be especially important in the third stage (chap. 4).

In terms of the historical materials, von Rad has said that no two holy wars are identical.[2] It may be better to say that no two reports of holy war are identical. Von Rad intended to point out that each holy war recorded in Scripture had a different configuration. These differences have led some scholars to deny any kind of uniform structure to the practice of holy

---

[2]G. von Rad, *Holy War in Ancient Israel* (1958; reprint, Grand Rapids: Eerdmans, 1991), 52.

war. We have to reckon, however, with the possibility that the difference has more to do with the high selectivity of biblical historical narrative than with a lack of coherence in holy war theory or practice.

With this in mind, we will describe holy war under three divisions: what takes place (1) before the war, (2) during the war, and (3) after the war.

BEFORE THE WAR

Seeking God's Will

Holy war was always initiated by Yahweh, never Israel. God did not agree to grant victory in every circumstance in which Israel found itself. There were two ways in which God directed Israel to wage war.

On some occasions, he revealed his will to the covenant mediator, who then informed the nation. This approach is illustrated by the conquest of the Promised Land. Among other places, God speaks to this effect in Deuteronomy 7:1-2:

> When the LORD your God brings you into the land you are entering to possess and drives out before you many nations—the Hittites, Girgashites, Amorites, Canaanites, Perizzites, Hivites and Jebusites, seven nations larger and stronger than you—and when the LORD your God has delivered them over to you and you have defeated them, then you must destroy them totally.

God makes his will vividly clear to the Israelites when the "commander of the army of the LORD" appears to Joshua on the eve of the destruction of Jericho (Jos 5:13–15). This episode recounts an unsolicited appearance of God to Joshua where the former not only commands Joshua to destroy the city, but also gives him a detailed battle strategy (Jos 6:2–5).

On the other hand, there were occasions when a battle situation arose and the war leader had to inquire of the Lord through oracular means. Such an incident is recorded in

1 Samuel 23:1–6, where David hears of the Philistine rape of the city of Keilah. David responds to the news by calling on the Lord. The Lord's answer is "Go, attack the Philistines and save Keilah." The means by which David inquired of the Lord is not directly specified, but it is relevant that the episode concludes with a parenthetical note: "Now Abiathar son of Ahimelech had brought the ephod down with him when he fled to David at Keilah." It is likely the ephod was used in oracular inquiries[3] and almost certainly was so used on this occasion.

An interesting counterexample is found in Joshua 9. Here the Gibeonites set up a ruse in order to trick Israel into thinking they were from outside of Palestine and thus not subject to complete destruction (Dt 20:16–18). The trick was successful, the text says, because the Israelites "did not inquire of the LORD" (Jos 9:14). The Lord, though, insisted that they honor the arrangement, but trouble later came to Israel because of their impetuous agreement (2Sa 23).

Spiritual Preparation

As odd as it may seem to modern sensibilities, battle is portrayed as an act of worship in the Hebrew Bible. The armies of Israel were in the presence of their God, and they had to be spiritually prepared for the experience. Unlike the teaching of the New Testament that God may be worshiped anywhere (Jn 4:21–24), during the period covered by the Hebrew Bible men and women could only encounter God in consecrated space. After the Fall (Ge 3), they could no longer simply approach God. Aware of their sin, they knew that certain steps were necessary to prevent their judgment. Sacrifice and ritual surrounded God's holiness, protecting worshipers from destruction.

---

[3]M. Haran, *Temples and Temple-Service in Ancient Israel* (Oxford: Clarendon Press, 1978), 214–15.

Since at the heart of holy war is God's presence with the army (see below), Israel had to be as spiritually prepared to go to battle as they would be to approach the sanctuary. This requirement explains many aspects of warfare in the Hebrew Bible, most notably the role of sacrifice. The importance of sacrifice prior to holy war is illustrated anecdotally by Saul's actions in 1 Samuel 13. This event caused alienation between Saul and Samuel (the latter was serving as the Lord's prophet). The issue between them centered on the sacrifices that took place before the battle; the controversy arose specifically when Saul offered the sacrifices in Samuel's stead. Apparently, Saul was guilty of usurping Samuel's priestly prerogatives. For our purposes, though, it suffices to point out that both Saul and Samuel agreed that sacrifices had to be offered before the commencement of battle. The narrative gives the impression that they were a necessary requirement.

The most impressive description of spiritual preparation before holy war is recorded in Joshua 5. This act was part of the process that was in response to Joshua's command to the people—"Consecrate yourselves" (*hiṭqaddāšû*; Jos 3:5).

On the eve of the battle against Jericho, the Israelite men were circumcised. Needless to say, this act was not wise from a military perspective. They were within marching distance of the powerful, hostile city, and circumcision would have left them weak and unable to defend themselves effectively (cf. Ge 34). Nonetheless, it would have been even more dangerous to enter the battle uncircumcised and therefore unclean before the Lord. After they were circumcised, the Israelites celebrated the Passover. Thus, when the battle began, they were ready to stand in the presence of the Lord.

The need for spiritual preparation is also evident in the story of David and Bathsheba (2Sa 11–12). After impregnating Bathsheba, David tries to cover up his transgression by calling her husband Uriah from the front lines of the Ammonite war, a war that David probably should have been leading. Twice

David tries to lure Uriah into the bed of his wife, but twice Uriah refuses. His refusal is based on his need to be spiritually prepared to reengage in holy war: "The ark and Israel and Judah are staying in the tents, and my master Joab and my lord's men are camped in the open fields. How could I go to my house to eat and drink and lie with my wife? As surely as you live, I will not do such a thing!" (2Sa 11:11). Uriah's concern is based on Leviticus 15:16–18, which describes a brief period of uncleanness after intercourse and calls for a washing ritual at the end of this period.

The contrast between David and Uriah is strong in this passage. David, the Lord's anointed, seeks to cover his sin of adultery by deception and finally by murder, while Uriah, a Hittite mercenary, honors Yahweh by staying at the ready by observing the customs of holy war.

Mention should also be made of the religious vows that the Bible records as taking place at least occasionally before a battle (Nu 21:2; Jdg 11:36; 1Sa 14:24). The exact status of those vows is difficult to assess, since in the last two passages the vows led to great grief in Israel, even though God honored the vows with victory.

Ritual Cleanness in the War Camp

A seemingly banal law in the book of Deuteronomy is actually charged with theological significance when seen in the light of holy war and the divine warrior. This law is found in Deuteronomy 23:9–14 and concerns the war camp.

The focus is on the need to preserve the ritual cleanness of the camp. Two specific instances are cited. In the first place, any warrior who ejaculates during the night must remove himself from the camp until he has gone through ritual purification.[4] The second case is what might be called the latrine law.

---

[4]A similar law is found in Leviticus 15:11–18, detailing the conditions of uncleanness occasioned by the emission of semen that would exclude the man from presence of the Lord.

Quite simply, the law states that it is inappropriate to have a latrine in the midst of the camp, and this for theological reasons: "For the LORD your God moves about your camp to protect you and to deliver your enemies to you" (Dt 23:14).

Conclusion

Many of the acts that preceded a war in the Hebrew Bible indicate the religious nature of the conflict. Sacrifice, circumcision, vows, oracular inquiries, ritual cleanness—each of these elements announced Israel's understanding that God was present with them in battle.

DURING THE WAR
Numbers and Weapons Technology

One of the most interesting aspects of holy war is the relationship between God and the Israelite army. Since God fights for Israel, that nation does not have to worry about the number of its troops or its weapons technology. Indeed, in the ethos of the Old Testament, a large army and superior weapons technology are a liability. Israel cannot boast in its own strength, but only in the power and might of the Lord, who gives victory in spite of overwhelming odds. It is better to go into battle with a small, poorly equipped army than with a large, well-trained one. Such concerns are behind the story of Gideon (Jdg 7). Thirty-two thousand men join him for battle. Yahweh, though, commands Gideon to pare down his army "in order that Israel may not boast against me that her own strength has saved her" (v. 2). Thus, he allows all the troops who are afraid to return home. Nonetheless, he still has ten thousand left. Finally, an apparently arbitrary test was set up so that only three hundred troops would be chosen to participate in the battle.

Perhaps the most striking illustration of these principles of holy war is found in the confrontation between David and Goliath (1Sa 17). These two men faced each other in individual combat as representatives of their respective nations.[5] The text leaves us wondering why the Philistines, who apparently had the upper hand, agreed to leave the outcome of the war to the results of this battle. We may speculate, however, that, while the Philistines knew they would ultimately win, they also realized that fighting Israel, lodged in the hill country, would be at heavy cost. They also had the likes of Goliath to depend on. Goliath was everything an ancient warrior could be: large, powerful, experienced, and armed with the most advanced weapons (17:4–7).

On the other hand, David was chosen for lack of an alternative. He was small and inexperienced in war. When he took the field, it was without armor, his only weapon being a simple slingshot. In this way, he is like Israel in holy war—outnumbered and inferior in weaponry. He also expresses the kind of holy war faith that Israel was called on to exhibit:

> You come against me with sword and spear and javelin, but I come against you in the name of the LORD Almighty, the God of the armies of Israel, whom you have defied. This day the LORD will hand you over to me, and I'll strike you down and cut off your head. Today I will give the carcasses of the Philistine army to the birds of the air and the beasts of the earth, and the whole world will know that there is a God in Israel. All those gathered here will know that it is not by sword or spear that the LORD saves; for the battle is the LORD's, and he will give all of you into our hands. (1Sa 17:45–47)

David then kills Goliath and cuts off his head.

---

[5]Such a battle of champions has ancient Near Eastern analogies. See Y. Yadin, *The Art of Warfare in Biblical Lands* (London: Weidenfeld and Nicolson, 1963), 265–67.

The March

Once the army was gathered and spiritually prepared, it marched into battle. In keeping with the relationship between worship and war, 2 Chronicles 20:20–23 describes the army singing praises to God during the march: "Give thanks to the LORD, for his love endures forever."

Psalm 149 may have also found its original setting in the march toward battle:

> May the praise of God be in their mouths
> and a double-edged sword in their hands,
> to inflict vengeance on the nations
> and punishment on the peoples,
> to bind their kings with fetters,
> their nobles with shackles of iron,
> to carry out the sentence written against them.
> This is the glory of all his saints. (vv. 6–9)

The ark played a prominent role in the march of early Israel. During the wilderness journey, the people of God were an army on the march toward battle. The ark, the emblem of God's presence (see below), led the wilderness generation just as the human king would lead his army on the march. Before the march began, Moses would say these words:

> Rise up, O LORD!
> May your enemies be scattered;
> may your foes flee before you. (Nu 10:35)

And then each night as the camp came to rest, Moses would proclaim:

> Return, O LORD
> to the countless thousands of Israel. (Nu 10:36)

The ark played an important role in the march toward battle, but the significance of the ark in war is much broader than that and deserves a separate discussion.

The Ark

Though God is an invisible spirit, he revealed himself to his people through a number of symbols, which indicated his presence. A selective survey of examples include a "smoking fire pot with a blazing torch" (Ge 15:17), a burning bush (Ex 3), and a cloud that filled the innermost room of the sanctuary (Ex 40:34–48). The tabernacle and the temple buildings successively symbolized God's presence in the midst of the Israelites. Even the furniture within these structures individually represented God's presence to his people. Carol Meyers' study of the tree symbolism of the menorah, ultimately hearkening back to the Garden of Eden, is a helpful example.[6] It can be argued, however, that among all of these symbols of God's presence, none occupied so important a place in the thinking of the Israelites as did the ark while it was in existence.[7]

The ark, as described in Exodus 25:10–22, was a simple wooden chest, made out of the precious wood of the acacia tree. It was normally housed in the Most Holy Place. From its description in Exodus, it sounds most like the footstool to God's throne. After all, Yahweh is said to meet with his people "above the cover between the two cherubim that are over the ark of the Testimony" (Ex 25:22).

Its connection with warfare, though, may be seen in its function as a mobile symbol of God's presence. The ark was constructed with four rings and two poles, so that it could be easily carried. Levites (Dt 10:8), specifically from the clan of Kohath (Nu 3:31; 4:5), were charged with transporting the ark from site to site during the wilderness trek. Above we cited the important passage in Numbers 10 that exposes the martial nature of the wilderness wanderings.

The ark represented the presence of God with the army during warfare. The very position of the ark in the camp shows

---

[6]C. L. Meyers, *The Tabernacle Menorah* (Missoula, Mont.: Scholars, 1976).

[7]M. H. Woudstra, *The Ark of the Covenant from Conquest to Kingship* (Phillipsburg, N.J.: Presbyterian and Reformed, 1965).

this. It led the army during the day and was placed in the Tent of Meeting located in the center of the camp at night (Nu 2). The ark was apparently carried into battle with the Israelite army. It is true that the ark is not mentioned in every battle narrative,[8] but this omission may be due in part to the early loss of the ark in the history of Israel and in part to the selective nature of biblical historiography.

Nonetheless, there are a number of stories in which the ark plays a prominent military role. Most notable is the central role of the ark in the drama surrounding the fall of Jericho during the period of the conquest. The instruction for the battle came from the divine warrior himself (Jos 5:13–15). The Israelite army was to march around the city once a day for six days, then on the seventh day to march around it seven times. The focus of attention, however, was not on the army, but rather on the ark in the middle of the army. Thus, the walls fell at the hand of God.

In a passage to be discussed in the next chapter, we can observe the importance of the ark in battle. When the Israelites had lost an initial encounter with the Philistines, Hophni and Phinehas insisted on carting the ark into the next battle (1Sa 4:4). At a later time, Uriah mentions that the ark was on the front lines of the battle against Ammon (2Sa 11:11).

The ark then functioned somewhat like the divine standard of the armies of the ancient Near East. It was a tangible representation of a spiritual reality—God's presence as divine warrior with his people.

The Combatants

Of course, according to biblical conceptions of God, he did not need Israel to fight in order to win the battle. Israel, however, is commanded to go to war. Thus, God and Israel

---

[8]G. H. Jones, "The Concept of Holy War," in *The World of the Old Testament*, ed. R. E. Clements (Cambridge, 1989), 299–322.

fought against the enemy together in holy war. The purpose of this section is to detail two more participants that Yahweh used in order to win the battle.

In the first place, there is an occasional mention of a heavenly army. This army was revealed to Elisha and his servant as they were apparently trapped in Dothan by the Aramean army. In response to Elisha's prayer, the text informs the reader that "the LORD opened the servant's eyes, and he looked and saw the hills full of horses and chariots of fire all around Elisha" (2Ki 6:17; see also Joel 2:11). The nature of this heavenly army is unclear in many references, but it is logical to think that the army was composed of angelic beings who belonged to the divine council.[9] Such a conception is supported by later apocalyptic texts that know of angelic beings who fight on behalf of God's people (Da 10:21;12:1; Rev 12:7).

The other ally of the divine warrior is the broader creation. Numerous accounts of holy war narrate God's use of aspects of nature in the battle. The account of the crossing at the Red Sea includes a description of God's use of "a strong east wind" (Ex 14:21) to separate the Red Sea, permitting the Israelites to pass through, but then also to destroy the Egyptian enemy. During the conquest, he destroyed the southern coalition of Canaanite cities by raining huge hailstones on their heads (Jos 10:9–11). In the context of the same battle, God stopped the sun and moon to permit the Israelites a longer day in order to complete their victory (Jos 10:1–15). Finally, in Deborah's song of praise to the Lord for victory over the Midianites, she mentions the part that creation played in the battle:

> Kings came, they fought;
>   the kings of Canaan fought
> at Taanach by the waters of Megiddo,
>   but they carried off no silver, no plunder.

---

[9]E. Th. Mullen, *The Divine Council in Canaanite and Early Hebrew Literature: The Assembly of the Gods,* HSM (Missoula, Mont.: Scholars, 1980).

From the heavens the stars fought,
   from their courses they fought against Sisera.
The river Kishon swept them away,
   the age-old river, the river Kishon. (Jdg 5:19–21)

Thus, God employed nature, his creation, as weapons in his battles.[10]

On the other hand, many passages of the Old Testament describe nature going into convulsions at the appearance of the divine warrior. His power and his might are so great that creation withers in his fearful presence. In particular, fertility ceases from the face of the earth (Isa 24:1–13; Mic 1:3, 4; Hab 3:6) and the seas dry up (Na 1:2–6; Hab 3:8). Nature's convulsions at the presence of God, the divine warrior, are partly explained by the Near Eastern background of the theme (see chap. 6).

AFTER THE BATTLE

Praise

If the battles were a divinely willed holy war, the conclusion was certain. God would deliver the enemy "into the hands" of Israel (Jos 6:2; 8:17, 18; 10:8, 19, 30; 11:8). The only proper response, upon recognition that the victory was God's gift to his people, was praise. The primary vehicle for that praise was song.

Two illustrations from the historical material will be sufficient. After the victory over the Egyptian forces at the Red Sea, Moses led Israel in a song of praise that celebrated the deliverance of Israel and the destruction of their enemies (Ex 15:1–18). This is followed by a brief song associated with Miriam:

---

[10]L. J. Greenspoon, "The Origin of the Idea of Resurrection," in *Traditions in Transformation*, ed. B. Halperin and J. D. Levenson (Winona Lake, Ind.: Eisenbrauns, 1981), 247–321.

Sing to the LORD,
    for he is highly exalted.
The horse and its rider
    he has hurled into the sea. (Ex 15:21)

The second example is from the period of the Judges and responds to the victory that the loosely confederated tribes of Israel won over the Canaanites. The song is associated with the leaders Deborah and Barak, and they thank God for his military victory:

O LORD, when you went out from Seir,
    when you marched from the land of Edom,
the earth shook, the heavens poured,
    the clouds poured down water.
The mountains quaked before the LORD, the One of Sinai,
    before the LORD, the God of Israel. (Jdg 5:4–5)

These historically specific psalms illustrate clearly the hymnic response to military victory. Close analysis of the Psalter reveals that a number of psalms also find their setting within the context of holy war. There were songs sung before a battle, calling on the Lord to "rise up" and defeat the enemy (Ps 7). Other psalms found a place in the camp during the respite of warfare, comforting the troops as they faced danger (Ps 91). Common are psalms that celebrate God's salvation ($y^e\check{s}\hat{u}^{\,\varsigma}\hat{a}$), better translated in most psalmic contexts as "deliverance" or "victory."

Psalm 98 is a concise example.[11] There are three stanzas. The first (vv. 1–3) thanks the Lord for his victory that has been accomplished in the past. The second (vv. 4–6) praises the Lord for his kingship in the present, while the third looks forward to his future judgment. As we will see, these three divine characteristics—warrior, king, and judge—are closely related.[12]

---

[11]T. Longman III, "Psalm 98: A Divine Warrior Victory Song," *JETS* 27 (1984): 267–74, and *How to Read the Psalms* (Downers Grove, Ill.: InterVarsity Press, 1988), 125–31.

[12]P. D. Miller, Jr., *The Divine Warrior in Early Israel* HSM, vol. 5 (Cambridge: Harvard University Press, 1973), 274.

There are many such psalms throughout the Psalter.[13] The psalms differ from our earlier examples because they are not historically specific.[14] That is, they do not celebrate any specific victory. Thus, they are models of victory prayers that may be used at different times throughout the period of the Old Testament.

At this point, we might add a word about the biblical phrase "new song." This phrase occurs in three biblical books, Isaiah (e.g., 42:10, 13), Psalms (40:3; 96:1; 98:1,3; 144:9; 149:1), and Revelation (5:5; 14:3). The close connection with warfare may be seen by quoting Psalm 144:9–10 (see also Ps 149, quoted on p. 39):

> I will sing a new song to you, O God;
>> on the ten-stringed lyre I will make music to you,
> to the One who gives victory to kings,
>> who delivers his servant David from the deadly sword.

It appears that "new song" is a technical term for victory song.[15] These songs celebrate the new situation brought about by God's warring activity.

This fits in with the broader issue of the connection between the divine warrior and music. Music ceases from the earth during the warring activity of God (Isa 24:4–13), but with victory music is renewed (Ps 98). In the historical books, women playing music greeted military leaders after a victory (Ex 15:21; Jdg 11:34).

The Plunder Belongs to the Lord

Since God won the victory, so the spoils of war belonged to him. The purest form of this is seen in the aftermath of the battle of Jericho. Everything was turned over to Yahweh:

---

[13]See Longman, "Psalm 98," for a list.

[14]Longman, *How to Read the Psalms*, 40–42.

[15]T. Longman III, "The Divine Warrior: The New Testament Use of an Old Testament Motif," *WTJ* 44 (1982): 300–302.

"Then they burned the whole city and everything in it, but they put the silver and gold and the articles of bronze and iron into the treasury of the LORD's house" (Jos 6:24). A well-known exception to this statement proves the rule. One person, Achan, tried to profit over the others by secreting some of the plunder into his tent. The defeat at Ai signaled that something was wrong in the war camp, and God quickly revealed the wrongdoer (Jos 7).

Other episodes are difficult to harmonize perfectly with what appears to be a principle that the war booty was turned over to the Lord. But even in a passage like 1 Samuel 30, where the plunder was divided among the troops, the rationale given for an even distribution between those soldiers who attacked the Amalekites and those who guarded the home base was that the plunder in actuality belonged to neither, but rather to the Lord (1Sa 30:23–25).

Ḥerem Warfare

The preceding discussion concerning the plunder of holy war leads directly to the concept of *ḥerem*.[16] *Ḥerem* is a Hebrew word that is variously translated as "banned" or "devoted things." It refers to plundered items and people who were captured during the course of a holy war.

The overarching principle of holy war is that God is present with his army. His army spiritually prepares for the encounter, but the same is not true of the enemy. Death is the only possible outcome. The aftermath of Jericho illustrates this: "They devoted the city to the LORD and destroyed with the sword every living thing in it—men and women, young and old, cattle, sheep and donkeys" (Jos 6:21).

---

[16]See P. D. Stern, *The Biblical* Herem: *A Window on Israel's Religious Experience*, BJS, vol. 211 (Atlanta: Scholars, 1991) for a detailed discussion.

A second textual example is found in 1 Samuel 15. Saul's problems with Yahweh and his representative Samuel began by mishandling the pre-battle sacrifices (1Sa 13). They came to a climax when Saul neglected to put the *ḥerem* into effect after a battle with the Amalekites. He took the flocks of the Amalekites as plunder, and he allowed Agag the king of the Amalekites to live. Samuel accused and then denounced Saul, taking on himself the task of executing the Amalekite king. This episode presages a growing rift between the kings who turned away from God and his commands concerning holy war and the prophets who became the primary bearers of holy war tradition (see the next chapter).

Conclusion: Yahweh the Divine Warrior

The above is a synthesis of legal and historical material surrounding holy war in Israel. Not every battle reflects this exact pattern. It is difficult to determine whether the differences are a variation of practice that evolved over time, or whether they are a function of the selectivity of biblical history writing. Probably both are involved. We have at least brushed the broad contours of the phenomenon of holy war in the Old Testament.

This chapter describes normative holy war. The central principle is that God is present in the battle with his people as a warrior. This is the origin of the divine-warrior theme, the experience of God's presence in battle. He wins the victory for his faithful people. This normative tradition applies throughout the Old Testament period, but primarily in the early history. As the kings grow distant from God, matters change. Warfare is no longer on behalf of Israel, but against Israel.

◆ 3 ◆

God Is an Enemy:
The Wars
Against Unfaithful Israel

God provided victory for Israel against Jericho, but in the very next battle Israel experienced a resounding defeat. The town of Ai was much smaller, an easier target than the large and well-defended Jericho. Nevertheless, the force that Joshua sent to destroy that town returned defeated and humiliated (Jos 7). God was Israel's divine warrior, so why were they defeated? What was the difference between Jericho and Ai?

THE DIVINE WARRIOR AND COVENANT

Behind God's actions as warrior stands the covenant.[1] God was in a covenant relationship with his people from the very start. By the time of Moses, there were already three covenant-making ceremonies recorded in the Bible, associated with Noah (Ge 9), Abraham (12:1–3; 15; 17), and Moses (Ex 19–24). The biblical concept of covenant, particularly as it pertains to the Mosaic covenant, has been elucidated by ancient

---

[1]Recent studies of the covenant include, O. P. Robertson, *The Christ of the Covenants* (Phillipsburg, N.J.: Presbyterian and Reformed, 1980); T. E. Mc-Comiskey, *The Covenants of Promise: A Theology of the Old Testament Covenants* (Grand Rapids: Baker, 1983).

Near Eastern treaties.[2] This analogy has enriched our understanding of covenant, so we now understand it to be a treaty between the divine king and his vassal people. In this covenant, God initiates a relationship of love and obedience. God makes promises to his people and expects them to respond by obeying his laws. These laws are sanctioned by blessings and curses. If his people obey the law, then they will be blessed, but they will be cursed if they neglect God and his requirements.

We see the relationship between the divine warrior and covenant in the blessings and curses of Deuteronomy (see also Lev 26:14–45). On the one hand, God promises his obedient covenant people that he will protect them against their enemies: "The LORD will grant that the enemies who rise up against you will be defeated before you. They will come at you from one direction but flee from you in seven" (Dt 28:7). On the other hand, the curses have in view a situation in which Israel is disobedient to its covenant Lord. In this case: "The LORD will cause you to be defeated before your enemies. You will come at them from one direction but flee from them in seven, and you will become a thing of horror to all the kingdoms on earth" (28:25). The present chapter focuses on the latter situations, the times in which Yahweh becomes Israel's enemy. We will begin by examining two texts: 1 Samuel 4:1–5:12 and the book of Lamentations. We will then examine the role of the prophets in connection with holy war, especially during periods of estrangement in the relationship between the king and God.

THE ARK: SYMBOL OF GOD'S PRESENCE OR MAGICAL TALISMAN?

First Samuel 4 and 5 narrate the story of the conflict between Israel and Philistia at the end of the judgeship of Eli. Israel's army was commanded by that weak leader's two corrupt

---

[2]M. G. Kline, *Treaty of the Great King* (Grand Rapids: Eerdmans, 1963).

sons, Hophni and Phinehas. The account begins with a short description of the defeat of the Israelite army at the hands of the Philistines at Aphek (4:1–2). In their post-battle analysis, the elders determined that their defeat was occasioned by the absence of the ark, which, as we observed above, was the primary symbol of God's presence.

The leaders of Israel thus sent for the ark. The dual response to the appearance of the ark in the Israelite camp illuminates the ark's function and ancient Near Eastern perceptions of the role of the divine in warfare. The Israelites shouted out, apparently in anticipation of victory. The Philistines reacted with fear. From their response, it is clear that they were aware of God's victories over the Egyptians during the Exodus. Having no other recourse, however, they determined to fight against Israel.

The battle and its consequences are briefly narrated and simply stated:

> So the Philistines fought, and the Israelites were defeated and every man fled to his tent. The slaughter was very great; Israel lost thirty thousand foot soldiers. The ark of God was captured, and Eli's two sons, Hophni and Phinehas, died. (1Sa 4:10–11)

The biblical narrator, as usual,[3] stays in the background and does not describe the motives of either the human or divine characters. The reader is left to read in the gaps to answer why Hophni and Phinehas' strategy failed. Fortunately, the next two episodes help us answer this question.

The first (1Sa 4:12–22) gives Shiloh's reaction to the defeat. A Benjamite survivor stumbled into the camp with the news that the army was defeated, Hophni and Phinehas dead,

---

[3]For studies of the role of the narrator in Hebrew prose stories, consult E. Auerbach, *Mimesis* (Princeton, N.J.: Princeton University Press, 1953), 3–23; R. Alter, *The Art of Biblical Narrative* (New York: Basic Books, 1981); and T. Longman III, *Literary Approaches to Biblical Interpretation* (Grand Rapids: Zondervan, 1987), 85–88.

and the ark captured. The most severe response came in answer to the last bit of information. Eli, the well-meaning yet incompetent judge, dropped over dead at the news. His unnamed daughter-in-law went into labor and gave birth to a boy. The naming of the child was fraught with significance for the theological interpretation of the story. He was Ichabod, meaning "No Glory." The daughter-in-law made explicit this meaning when she interpreted: "The glory has departed from Israel, for the ark of God has been captured" (4:22).

The next scene makes it clear that Israel lost the battle in spite of the presence of the ark, not because God was unable to defeat the Philistines, but because he was unwilling. The setting shifts to Philistia itself where the victors had taken the ark and placed it in the presence of their chief god, Dagon. Our understanding of similar situations elsewhere in the ancient Near East leads us to the conclusion that the Philistines likely venerated Yahweh as a potent, yet subordinate deity to Dagon. The text, though, simply says that they placed the ark "beside Dagon." The preposition "beside" ('$\bar{e}\d{s}el$) does not itself denote subordination,[4] and it may be that the Philistines themselves thought they were honoring this foreign deity.

Yahweh, however, recognizes no other deities as rivals. He thus displayed his power before the Philistines and over Dagon. The morning after the ark was introduced into the temple of Dagon, the latter's priests discovered the statue of Dagon fallen on its face in front of Yahweh. The Philistines had placed the ark in the temple as a kind of trophy of Dagon, and the next day Dagon was prostrate (as if in worship) before the ark. The reaction of the Philistines is not given at this point; it is simply reported that the priests put Dagon back in his place. Any thought, however, that Dagon's fall was the result of chance was removed the next day when he was fallen once

---

[4]See Waltke and O'Connor, *An Introduction to Biblical Hebrew Syntax* (Winona Lake, Ind.: Eisenbrauns, 1989), 11.2.3.

again, this time with damage. Dagon's head and hands were severed, perhaps on analogy with the practice of removing the heads and hands of vanquished enemies.

Along with the events inside the temple of Dagon, God also loosed a plague in the Philistine city of Ashdod (1Sa 5:6–8). Once again, the Philistines guarded against the possibility that this plague was chance, so they moved the ark to Gath (5:8b–10a). The Philistines finally perceived the significance of these events when the plague followed the ark to the third town, Ekron (5:10b–12), and they returned the ark to the Israelites (6:1–7:1). The Israelites and later readers should also get the point. The reason for the ark's failure to deliver Israel from Philistia was not because of divine inability but because of divine unwillingness. God would not fight on behalf of an apostate Israel. Indeed, he would become its enemy.

THE EXILE

The reflex of the Exodus is the Exile. If the Exodus shows God's power on behalf of Israel, the Exile displays God's power against Israel. The Exodus is an expression of God's grace; the Exile displays his judgment. In the Exodus event we witness God as Israel's warrior; in the Exile, he is Israel's enemy.

DIVINE ABANDONMENT

Israel felt secure since God dwelt in its midst. The temple, God's house on earth, was the primary symbol of his presence. This is the message of the so-called Zion theology as expressed in Psalm 46:

> There is a river whose streams make glad the city of God,
>> the holy place where the Most High dwells.
> God is within her, she will not fall;
>> God will help her at break of day.

> Nations are in uproar, kingdoms fall;
>> he lifts his voice, the earth melts.
> The LORD Almighty is with us;
>> the God of Jacob is our fortress. (vv. 4–7)

No nation could defeat Israel. God was in its midst to protect it.

Israel, however, presumed upon God's presence and protection. The nation often turned its back on its Lord. The Deuteronomic history contains a catalogue of sins against God, the most heinous of which was idolatry.

According to Jeremiah, Israel took God's protecting presence for granted, even on the eve of the Exile. Jeremiah charges the people of God with sinning continually but still counting on the Lord to save them. He mimics their chant (7:4): "The temple of the LORD, the temple of the LORD, the temple of the LORD!" The temple was a tangible sign that God was in their midst, so the city could not be defeated. It was not the temple, however, but God who served as Israel's defense. The burden of Jeremiah 7 is that this trust in the temple was not supported by true faith in God or a lifestyle of obedience.

Ezekiel describes God's reaction to the apostasy of his people: He has abandoned his temple. The first step was God removal from the Holy of Holies, where he was enthroned above the ark, to the threshold of the temple (Eze 9:3). As he moved, he gave orders that led to the destruction of those among his people who had not obeyed him.

In Ezekiel 10 God moved outside the temple to the waiting cherubim. The description of the vehicle here and in Ezekiel 1 is difficult to reconstruct. There seems little doubt, though, that the text is describing some type of chariot, with the cherubim functioning like horses. In any case, God mounted the cherubim-driven vehicle (10:18), which immediately took to the air. He stopped momentarily at the east gate of the temple complex (10:19). In the next chapter, however, God's glory departed the city, heading east (11:23). It is probably no coincidence that Babylon was directly east of Israel.

Later, readers likely inferred that God was going to Babylon in order to prepare that country to serve as the instrument of divine judgment against God's own people. After all, Habakkuk represented God as saying: "I am raising up the Babylonians, that ruthless and impetuous people, who sweep across the whole earth to seize dwelling places not their own" (Hab 1:6). Jeremiah too saw God's hand closely associated with the Babylonian attack on Judah and Jerusalem:

> But Jeremiah answered them, "Tell Zedekiah, 'This is what the LORD, the God of Israel, says: I am about to turn against you the weapons of war that are in your hands, which you are using to fight the king of Babylon and the Babylonians who are outside the wall besieging you. And I will gather them inside this city. I myself will fight against you with an outstretched hand and a mighty arm in anger and fury and great wrath. I will strike down those who live in this city—both men and animals—and they will die of a terrible plague. After that, declares the LORD, I will hand over Zedekiah king of Judah, his officials and the people in this city who survive the plague, sword, and famine, to Nebuchadnezzar king of Babylon and to their enemies who seek their lives. He will put them to the sword; he will show them no mercy or pity or compassion.'" (21:3–7)

DIVINE HOSTILITY

The last passage goes beyond divine abandonment and points to divine hostility, God's acting against Israel in warfare. Language that in other places was used in support of Israel is here applied against Israel. The "outstretched hand" and the "mighty arm" are turned against his people (cf. Ex 6:6; Dt 4:34; Ps 136:12). He will "hand over" Israel to its enemies (cf. Jos 11:6; Jdg 4:9; 1Sa 17:46).

The most desperate expression of the ravages of God's hostility may be found in the book of Lamentations. The contents and tone of this biblical book are in the tradition of ancient Near Eastern laments over the destruction of a city. The two best-known examples are the Sumerian texts "Lamentation over the Destruction of Ur"[5] and "Lamentation over the Destruction of Sumer and Ur."[6] While there is no direct connection between the Sumerian compositions and the biblical text—which, after all, was composed over a millennium later—the connections do "illustrate the persistence of ancient literary motifs into late biblical literature."[7]

The unnamed author of this poignant grief psalm looks at the destruction that surrounds him in Jerusalem and sees, not Babylonian aggression, but divine hostility:

> The Lord is like an enemy;
> he has swallowed up Israel.
> He has swallowed up her palaces
> and destroyed her strongholds.
> He has multiplied mourning and lamentation
> for the Daughter of Judah. (La 2:5)

The Exile is the culmination and most fearsome expression of what might be called "reverse holy war."[8] God wars against his own people to punish them for their disobedience.

THE PROPHETS AND HOLY WAR DURING PERIODS OF ROYAL APOSTASY

From the inception of the kingship in Israel, the prophets acted as the divinely commissioned royal conscience. The relationship between the prophet and the king may be aptly illustrated by the role of Samuel at the time of Saul's coronation. Up to that moment, Samuel had functioned as both

---

[5] *ANET*, 455–63.

[6] *ANET*, 611–19.

[7] D. R. Hillers, *Lamentations*, AB (Garden City, N.Y.: Doubleday, 1972), xxx.

[8] W. L. Moran, "The End of the Unholy War and the Anti-Exodus," *Bib* 44 (1963): 333–42.

religious and political leader in Israel. Due to foreign threats to Israel's independence (1Sa 8:19–20), the people wanted a king to rule over them and direct their armies. Samuel recognized this desire as criticism of his leadership, but the deeper problem was a lack of trust in God as divine warrior (8:6–9). Nevertheless, kingship itself was not an inherently wicked institution; it had been anticipated long before the time of Samuel (Ge 17:16; Dt 17:14–20). Thus, God approved of the establishment of the monarchy (1Sa 8:22), and Samuel set out to find the right person.

The next three chapters (1Sa 9–11) narrate the rise of Saul to the kingship, but the section climaxes in the twelfth chapter with a covenant renewal. This ceremony was necessary because the covenant relationship had been threatened by the nature of the people's request[9] and the nature of the kingship. The human king was to be subordinate to the heavenly king (Dt 17:14–20) and a reflection of the divine glory. It would be tempting, however, for the people and for the king himself to consider the king as sovereign and in the place of God (1Sa 8:10–18).

During this renewal ceremony, Samuel established himself, and by implication the line of prophets who followed him, as spokesperson for the heavenly king/court/divine council (cf. Michaiah in 1Ki 22). In so doing, he envisioned the possibility that the king as well as the people would sin:

> As for me, far be it from me that I should sin against the LORD by failing to pray for you. And I will teach you the way that is good and right. But be sure to fear the LORD and serve him faithfully with all your heart; consider what great things he has done for you. Yet if you persist in doing evil, both you and your king will be swept away. (1Sa 12:23–25)

---

[9]J. R. Vannoy, *Covenant Renewal at Gilgal* (Cherry Hill, N.J.: Mack Publishing, 1977).

The Saul narrative that follows gives ample illustration of Samuel's new role. In the next chapter, Samuel had to reprimand Saul for holy war violations. The result was that, while he allowed Saul to continue his rule, God would not establish his dynasty (1Sa 13:14). That was not, however, the only conflict between Saul and Samuel. The rift broadened after Saul defeated the Amalekites but failed to put the ban into effect (1Sa 15:13–33). Saul's punishment was the loss of the kingship (1Sa 15:26) and a permanent estrangement with Samuel (15:35).

Thus, we observe that one aspect of the prophet's role was to be the king's conscience. Von Rad recognized this when he stated that the Saul-Samuel relationship "is proof that the prophetic movement understood itself as custodian of the patriarchal order of the Holy War."[10] When a king departed from the way of the Lord, it was the duty of the prophet to confront him.

The story of Saul and Samuel illustrates another point in the relationship between the king and the prophet. When a king turned against the Lord, it was the prophet and not the king who performed holy war and was the beneficiary of God's warring activity. When Saul refused to execute Agag according to the requirements of the *herem*, Samuel himself took a sword and hacked him to pieces (1Sa 15:33). Thus, often during times of royal apostasy God turned against the king and the people who followed him as divine warrior and toward the prophets and his faithful followers.

The ministry of Elijah and Elisha during the Omride dynasty is a case in point. Ahab, under the influence of Jezebel, his foreign queen, turned away from the pure worship of Yahweh to a syncretistic form of worship that included the worship of Baal. Baal was the head of the Canaanite pantheon and was the god of the rain and dew, and of fertility in general.

---

[10]G. von Rad, *Holy War in Ancient Israel* (1958; reprint, Grand Rapids: Eerdmans, 1991), 97.

God's reaction to Ahab's apostasy was to strike at the nation precisely in the area of Baal's specialty by afflicting the land with a drought (1Ki 17:1). God fought against the Israelite king and not for him.

The Ahab narrative is generated by conflict–a conflict between Elijah and Ahab on a human level, and on the divine level between God and Baal.[11] First Kings 18 is a case in point. Here God instructed Elijah to confront Ahab and the Baal priesthood. He challenged them, and through them Baal, to a contest. The object of the contest was the lighting of the sacrificial fires. Whichever god lit the fire won, and thereby proved his existence.

The account of this conflict is one of the most dramatic in the Bible. Everything was against Elijah. In the first place, he was in a decided minority. He stood alone against four hundred and fifty prophets of Baal and four hundred prophets of Asherah. Second, they went first. If the altar fire was lit, the contest was over. Third, the contest was in the area of Baal's "specialty." In a polytheistic religious system, the deities each have their areas of expertise. In the case of Baal, besides being the chief god of the pantheon, he was, as mentioned, also the god of rain and fertility. As part of his sovereignty over rain, he was also in charge of lightning, throwing fire from the sky (1Ki 18:24).

Ahab then instructed his prophets to call on Baal to set fire to the sacrifice, but after numerous attempts nothing happened. Elijah took the opportunity to mock Baal and his worshipers (1Ki 18:27). Then, in response to Baal's absence, the prophets gashed themselves, reflecting an act that the god El performed when Baal had been devoured by Mot (KTU 1.5 vi).

The action then shifts to Elijah. After repairing the Yahweh altar on Mount Carmel, he took further steps to demonstrate

---

[11]L. Bronner, *The Stories of Elijah and Elisha as Polemics against Baal Worship* (Leiden: Brill, 1968).

the presence and power of Yahweh by pouring water over all the sacrifice and the wood under it (1Ki 18:33–35). Thus, when Yahweh responded with fire from heaven and lit the fire, there would be no doubt about its divine origin.

Elijah then called on the Lord with a simple prayer, not the apparently dramatic invocation of the Baal prophets (cf. v. 26 with vv. 36–37). Yahweh's response was immediate and overwhelming (cf. v. 38 with v. 26). The episode leaves the reader in the same position as the original witnesses to the event—with no doubt about the power and superiority of Yahweh (v. 39).

First Kings 18 illustrates our point that during times of apostasy God aided his prophets over against the king. Second Kings 6:8–23 specifically shows Yahweh as divine warrior protecting his prophets against danger. As the episode opens, the Arameans have declared war against Israel. God, though, enlightened Elijah concerning the enemy's strategy, and the prophet kept the king informed of Aramean movements. The king of Aram suspected a spy, but one of his officers knew the real source of the trouble—Elisha, the man of God. Thus, the Aramean king moved against the unarmed prophet by attacking his home in Dothan, situated in the plain just below the imposing Mount Carmel.

One morning the prophet and his band woke up to discover a huge army around the city. Elisha's servant panicked on seeing the army, realizing that they were not equipped to defend themselves. Elisha remained calm, apparently because he understood the spiritual reality of the situation. He asked God to open his servant's eyes, and when he did, the servant saw "the hills full of horses and chariots of fire" (v. 17). This army was obviously the celestial army of God, ready to fight on behalf of the prophet.

It is interesting to note, though, that the celestial army did not move into actual battle with the Arameans. Rather, the Arameans were struck blind as they attacked the prophet.

Thus, Elisha was able to lead them into the heart of Samaria and allowed the king of Israel to trap them.

CONCLUSION: GOD AS AN ENEMY

In this chapter, we have seen that God was not at Israel's beck and call in warfare. He would not provide the victory for them in any and every situation. They had to obey the covenant; otherwise, they were liable to God's judgment. At such times God turned against Israel as an enemy. This reversal of holy war came about particularly when the king trusted his weapons more than the Lord (Isa 30:15–16; Amos 2:13–16). We observed this reversal at the time of Hophni and Phinehas; we also noted how the divine warrior supported and fought for the prophets at times when the king neglected his religious duties. We are not to think, however, that there was a radical turn at some point in Israel's history. When there were obedient kings, God fought on their behalf even down to the eve of the Exile (2Ch 20). But the Exile was the watershed. The Babylonian incursion and resultant exile were the culmination of God's warlike activity against his own people. Even in the following period of restoration, God did not fight for his people against their flesh-and-blood enemies. Rather, a whole new phase of God's warrior activity began with late Old Testament prophets like Zechariah and Daniel.

◆ 4 ◆

God Will Come:
The Day of the Lord

The destruction of Jerusalem and the Babylonian exile marked the end of an era. Israel was bereft of political independence and power for the remainder of biblical history. God no longer fought for Israel's king and army, because Israel no longer had a king or an army.

Nevertheless, God did not completely abandon his people. The prophets could see his hand behind history as Persia under Cyrus dislodged the Babylonians from world domination. The Persians had a different foreign policy,[1] and they permitted peoples who were exiled by the Babylonians to return to their lands, the Israelites included. Thus, under such leaders as Sheshbazzar, Zerubbabel, Ezra, and Nehemiah, the remnant of the people of God resettled Jerusalem and the surrounding area.

Nonetheless, they were still a subjugated people without an independent government. They were one province among many in the Persian empire. Furthermore, no longer were the Israelites exclusively resident in Israel; there were faithful

---

[1]P. Ackroyd, *Exile and Restoration* (Philadelphia: Westminster, 1968), 140–41.

people of God throughout the empire, even at its center of power (Esther). In this new context, what did it mean that God was a warrior? We will answer this question by a close examination of two representative biblical texts of the late Old Testament period: Daniel 7 and Zechariah 14.

THE RISE OF APOCALYPTIC IN ISRAEL

Both Daniel 7 and Zechariah 14 may be classified as apocalyptic literature. Thus, before closely examining these two passages, it will be helpful to discuss Old Testament apocalyptic in general. As we will see, the two most prominent motifs of this genre of biblical literature are the divine warrior and the closely related Day of the Lord.

As with most genre distinctions, apocalyptic is a debated category with fuzzy boundaries. It was only in the early nineteenth century that Frederick Lücke[2] introduced the term to describe a particular type of prophetic writing. The primary representative of the genre was the book of Revelation, and Lücke named the genre after the first word of that book (*apokalupsis*). Accordingly, any book that bore significant similarity with Revelation was grouped in this new genre. Within the biblical corpus, only Daniel bore an undeniable comparison to Revelation, though a number of intertestamental books (e.g., Enoch) accompanied them. There were, in addition, a number of Old Testament books whose exact generic connection was debated: parts of Isaiah, Zechariah, Joel, and Zephaniah among others.

Indeed, debate continues on the whole issue of the nature and scope of apocalyptic. The genre is fluid and must be seen on a continuum with prophecy and not as a completely distinct literary genre. Space does not permit us to present the ar-

---

[2]F. Lücke, *Versuch einer vollständigen Einleitung in die Offenbarung Johannis und die gesammte apokalyptische Litteratur* (Bonn: Weber, 1832).

guments here,[3] but the following Old Testament texts demonstrate the cluster of traits that we associate with apocalyptic[4]: Isaiah 24–27, Daniel, Joel, Zephaniah, and Zechariah.

THE DIVINE WARRIOR THEME IN APOCALYPTIC

An examination of the above-mentioned apocalyptic texts indicates that the divine warrior is a major theme in apocalyptic. All of them describe God as a warrior who does battle with his enemies on behalf of his people. We will now closely read two illustrative texts: Daniel 7 and Zechariah 14.

DANIEL 7: GOD BATTLES THE FOUR MONSTERS FROM THE SEA

In the first place, we may divide the chapter into two parts: the dream (vv. 1–14) and its interpretation (vv. 15–28). Our attention will be centered on the first half, but of course, we will appeal to the interpretation of the dream to guide our understanding of the vision.

The dream itself is composed of two sections. The first is a metaphoric description of evil (vv. 1–8). The setting is presented in Daniel 7:2, the first verse of the dream. It is a sea shore at a time when the waves are whipped to a frenzy by the winds coming from four different directions.

---

[3]The leading antagonists in the debate over the nature and scope of apocalyptic are P. D. Hanson, *The Dawn of Apocalyptic* (Philadelphia: Fortress, 1975); J. J. Collins, *Apocalypse: The Morphology of a Genre, Semeia* 14 (Missoula, Mont.: Scholars, 1979); and C. Rowland, *The Open Heaven: A Study of Apocalyptic in Judaism and Early Christianity* (New York: Crossroad, 1982). Other works include J. Carmignac, "Qu'est-ce que l'Apocalyptique? Son emploi à Qumran," *RevQ* 37 (1979): 3–33; W. R. Millar, *Isaiah 24–27 and the Origin of Apocalyptic,* HSM, vol. 11 (Missoula, Mont.: Scholars, 1976).

[4]See T. Longman III, *Fictional Akkadian Autobiography* (Winona Lake, Ind.: Eisenbrauns, 1991), 167–84 for a list and discussion of these traits.

By the time of Daniel 7, the sea is a well-established image for the realm of chaos.[5] The psalms contain a number of allusions to the struggle between God and the sea. In Psalm 18 the composer thanks God for saving him from his distress. In the process he recounts a theophany during which:

> The valleys of the sea were exposed
>   and the foundations of the earth laid bare
> at your rebuke, O LORD,
>   at the blast of breath from your nostrils. (Ps 18:15)[6]

Other descriptions of the conflict between God and the sea may be discovered in the following passages (the specific action of God toward the sea is in parentheses—the list is from Kloos):

Jeremiah 5:22; Job 7:12 ("to establish a border, to set a guard")
Isaiah 19:5; 50:2; Jeremiah 51:36; Ezekiel 30:12; Nahum 1:4; Psalm 18:16 [=2 Samuel 22:16]; Job 12:15 ("to dry up")
Habakkuk 3:15 ("to tread upon")
Isaiah 27:1 ("to fight the monsters")[7]

As is well known, this biblical image is connected with the Near Eastern myth that narrates the struggle between the Sea and the chief deity of a pantheon. In the Ugaritic myths we read of Baal's struggles against Yam ("the sea") and his henchmen, including the seven-headed Lotan (= Leviathan). According to Jacobsen,[8] the Mesopotamian reflex of this story comes from Syria and is observed most notably in the *Enuma Elish*.[9] In this tale, Marduk steps forward to battle Tiamat,

---

[5]M. K. Wakeman, *God's Battle with the Monster. A Study in Biblical Imagery* (Leiden: Brill, 1973); J. Day, *God's Conflict with the Dragon and the Sea* (Cambridge: Cambridge University Press, 1975).

[6]Similar sentiments may be discovered in Psalm 29:3; Isaiah 1:2; Nahum 1:4; and Habakkuk 3:8.

[7]C. Kloos, *Yhwh's Combat with the Sea: A Canaanite Tradition in the Religion of Ancient Israel* (Leiden: Brill, 1986), 81–83.

[8]T. Jacobsen, "The Battle Between Marduk and Tiamat," *JAOS* 88 (1968): 104–8.

[9]*ANET*, 60–62.

whose name means Sea. He establishes himself as chief of the gods by his victory and proceeds to create the world out of her body. There appears to be the constant threat of a reversion to this anticreation chaos, since the *Enuma Elish* concludes with "a prayer that the violence of her flood threat shall continue to be restrained for another year at least."[10]

To repeat our earlier assertion, the sea was a symbol of the forces of chaos, standing over against creation and the agent of creation, God. Thus, the sea setting in Daniel 7:2 itself creates a sense of foreboding and fear for what is to come.

Four beasts arise in succession out of the chaotic sea. The first characteristic of these beasts that strikes the reader is their hybrid nature. With the exception of the third beast, they are combinations of different creatures. The first beast, for instance, combines the traits of an eagle, a lion, and a man. The modern reader should realize the tremendous revulsion that the description of these beasts would likely have stirred in the minds of the original readers. Two lines of evidence indicate the Israelite reader's strong reaction to the mixed character of these beasts. The first is the creation story. Here God made the various components of his creation "according to their ... kinds" (*l^e mînô*: Ge 1:11–12, 21, 24–25); the different parts of creation were created to be unique and separate. Second, the Israelite concern with separation of species was embedded in their laws, which indicated that the original creation order was to be preserved through history. A series of laws in Deuteronomy 22:9–11 is a case in point. "Do not plant two kinds of seed in your vineyard; if you do, not only the crops you plant but also the fruit of the vineyard will be defiled. Do not plow with an ox and a donkey yoked together. Do not wear clothes of wool and linen woven together." Thus, the four beasts that arise from the chaotic sea are natural images of grotesque horror to the original Israelite readers.

---

[10]N. Forsyth, *The Old Enemy: Satan and the Combat Myth* (Princeton: Princeton University Press, 1987), 49.

The next question to be answered is what these beasts symbolized in their historical setting. The interpreting angel gives a general answer to this question in Daniel 7:17: "The four great beasts are four kingdoms that will rise from the earth." The difficulty is to identify properly the specific referent of the symbolism of the four beasts. Traditionally, they have been taken as Babylon, Medo-Persia, Greece, and Rome. Good arguments can be marshaled in support of this approach. Critical scholarship, however, has had its doubts,[11] especially with the identification of the fourth beast as Rome. After all, according to critical understanding, the book was written toward the middle of the second century B.C.E. and would more naturally conclude with Greece. Thus, an alternative identification is Babylon, Media, Persia, Greece. It should be pointed out that such a pattern is argued today by some evangelical scholars, though on different grounds.[12]

While this is an important and interesting issue, it is not of critical importance to our concern. What is significant is the conflict that exists between these four beasts (as well as the horns associated with the fourth) and the two figures in the second half of the vision: "the Ancient of Days" and the "one like a son of man."

Our first impression as we read the second half of the vision is that we have gone up the "chain of being," so to speak. That is, while the evil kingdoms of this world are imaged by Daniel as animals, so the divine realm is pictured as humanlike. This association is perfectly appropriate in a broader biblical view because, after all, Genesis 1:28 tells us that God created men and women in his own image.

---

[11]H. H. Rowley, *Darius the Mede and the Four World Empires in the Book of Daniel* (San Diego, Calif.: Cardiff, 1935).

[12]R. J. M. Gurney, *God in Control: An Exposition of the Prophecies of Daniel* (Worthing: Walter, 1980); J. H. Walton, "The Four Kingdoms of Daniel," *JETS* 29 (1986): 25–36.

The first figure is called the "Ancient of Days." The context makes it abundantly clear that this figure is divine. He is God, specifically in his role as judge. As such, he is imaged as an old and presumably wise human judge sitting in his court room. The second figure, "one like a son of man," is more startling in its Old Testament context. This figure is obviously divine. After all, he is riding the cloud chariot that is the prerogative of God alone.

Like the image of the sea, the image of the cloud rider was an ancient one by the time we come to Daniel 7:13. Cloud imagery associated with the Lord's appearance is as old as the Exodus and the pillar of cloud by day and the fire by night (Ex 13:21). During the climactic theophany on Sinai, the mountain was covered by a cloud (19:16). In the tabernacle, God appeared in the cloud that was present in the Holy of Holies (Lev 16:2).

We learn of the vehicular cloud, however, in the psalms and the prophets. God is the cloud rider in Psalm 68:4:

> Sing to God, sing praise to his name,
> > extol him who rides on the clouds
> his name is the LORD—
> > and rejoice before him.

and in Psalm 104:3-4:

> He makes the clouds his chariot
> > and rides on the wings of the wind.
> He makes winds his messengers,
> > flames of fire his servants.

The prophets also use the cloud-riding image in clear judgment/war contexts:

> See, the LORD rides on a swift cloud
> > and is coming to Egypt.
> The idols of Egypt tremble before him,
> > and the hearts of the Egyptians melt within them. (Isa 19:1)

> The LORD is slow to anger and great in power;
>> the LORD will not leave the guilty unpunished.
> His way is in the whirlwind and the storm,
>> and clouds are the dust of his feet. (Na 1:3)

Like the sea image, God's riding clouds also has an ancient Near Eastern background. This connection may be most closely observed in the literature from Ugarit. Baal, the chief deity and primary divine warrior of that culture, is often called the "Rider on the Clouds." Indeed, it is one of his most common epithets:

> "Hearken, O Puissant Baal:
> Give heed, O Rider on the Clouds."[13]

This example could be multiplied many times. Baal was the god of the thunderstorm in the Ugaritic pantheon. His cloud riding was appropriate to his function.

Thus, Daniel 7:1–14 presents the reader with two image clusters. On the one hand, we have four beasts and horns that represent depraved human kingdoms; on the other hand, we see two human figures, the Ancient of Days and one like a son of man, who image the divine realm.

According to the angelic interpreter, there is war between the beasts, particularly the final horn, and "the saints of the Most High" (v. 18). The debate surrounding the exact referent of this latter phrase is intense. The most natural reading though is that they are the faithful people of God. The passage describes the struggle and looks forward to the future intervention of God, the divine warrior:

> As I watched, this horn was waging war against the saints and defeating them, until the Ancient of Days came and pronounced judgment in favor of the saints of the Most High, and the time came when they possessed the kingdom. (vv. 21–22)

---

[13]*ANET*, 134.

But the court will sit, and his power will be taken away
and completely destroyed forever. Then the sovereignty,
power and greatness of the kingdoms under the whole
heaven will be handed over to the saints, the people of the
Most High. His kingdom will be an everlasting kingdom,
and all rulers will worship and obey him. (vv. 26–27)

In other words, Daniel 7 paints a picture of a human
struggle, which is also a cosmic struggle. It presents hope to
the oppressed readers that God will come in the future to save
his people from their apparently overwhelming enemies.

ZECHARIAH 14

The authorship and date of this chapter have been con-
tested, but its present canonical setting associates this oracle
with Zechariah, a post-exilic prophet. Like Daniel before him,
Zechariah presents a vision of a future violent intervention of
God.

The chapter begins with a reference to a coming "day of
the LORD" (14:1). The significance of the phrase "day of the
LORD" (Isa 13:6, 9; Joel 1:15; 2:1, 11; Am 5:8–20; Zep 1:7–8) is
a debated subject. S. Mowinckel argued that the phrase and
the concept behind it belonged to the ritual of the New Year's
Festival.[14] Increasingly, however, scholars are recognizing that
Mowinckel's New Year Festival of enthronement was based on
a faulty analogy with Babylonian texts, for the Old Testament
does not support such a construction. Early on, G. von Rad argued that the concept of the "Day of Yahweh encompasses a
pure event of war."[15] Specifically, he persuasively linked the
Day of the Lord with early Israelite Holy War tradition. Furthermore, his conclusion held even if one did not accept his
method of starting the investigation with Isaiah 13; 24; Ezekiel

---

[14]S. Mowinckel, *He That Cometh* (Oxford: Basil Blackwell, 1956), 132–33.
[15]G. von Rad, "The Origin of the Concept of the Day of Yahweh," *JSS* 4
(1959): 97–108, especially p. 103.

7; and Joel 2 or agree with the manner in which he restricted his study to phrases that use only the words *Day of the Lord*.[16] F. M. Cross, while in some respects mediating between Mowinckel and von Rad, arrived at the same conclusion—that the Day of Yahweh was grounded in Holy War tradition.[17] In any case, as D. Stuart points out in his study of the extrabiblical background of the phrase, there is a clear connection between the *yom Yahweh* and military language.[18]

Thus, the opening verse sets the tone of what follows, a great battle. The second verse describes an attack on Jerusalem. The situation looks dire. But then the divine warrior appears with his heavenly army: "The LORD will go out and fight against those nations, as he fights in the day of battle.... Then the LORD my God will come, and all the holy ones with him" (Zec 14:3, 5). The rest of the chapter describes the cosmic and societal upheaval that results from the appearance of the divine warrior. The result is the Lord's victory over the nations and the exaltation of Jerusalem. The end of the chapter looks forward to a day when Jerusalem will be like the temple precincts:

> On that day HOLY TO THE LORD will be inscribed on the bells of the horses, and the cooking pots in the LORD's house will be like the sacred bowls in front of the altar. Every pot in Jerusalem and Judah will be holy to the LORD Almighty, and all who come to sacrifice will take some of the pots and cook in them. And on that day there will no longer be a Canaanite in the house of the LORD Almighty. (Zec 14:20–21)

---

[16]Concerning these methodological questions, see most recently Y. Hoffmann, "The Day of the Lord as a Concept and a Term in the Prophetic Literature," *ZAW* 93 (1981): 37–50.

[17]F. M. Cross, "The Divine Warrior," in *Canaanite Myth and Hebrew Epic* (Cambridge: Harvard University Press, 1973), 91–111; see also P. D. Miller, Jr., "The Divine Council and the Prophetic Call to War," *VT* 18 (1968): 100–107.

[18]D. Stuart, "The Sovereign's Day of Conquest," *BASOR* 221 (1976): 159–64.

Thus, Zechariah concludes with a vision of the future, a vision that looks forward to a coming intervention of the divine warrior. The present and near future are dire times for the people of God, but God will have the last word. He will come and save his oppressed people from their distress.

CONCLUSION

This message of future deliverance is the note on which the Old Testament draws to a close. The divine warrior had protected them in the past. Their present situation was the result of his punishing wrath, but the future held the certain hope that God would return once again as a mighty warrior to save them.

♦ 5 ♦

God Wars Against the Forces of Chaos

The previous three chapters described God's warfare on the historical plane. In this chapter we will explore biblical data that suggests that there is war on the suprahistorical plane as well, that is, warfare between spiritual beings that is not restricted to the earthly plane. As we will see below, however, the historical and suprahistorical, the earthly and the heavenly, are not isolated from each other. They are integrally connected.

Perhaps even more than in previous chapters, our approach to the Bible affects our conclusions in this chapter. This is true both in terms of our understanding of the development of biblical books as well as the relationship between them. It also concerns our explanation of the obvious connection between biblical books. (For a brief description of this approach and references to more detailed studies, see pp. 26–27.)

THE CONFLICT BEGINS

As observed in chapter 2, the divine warrior theme does not become explicit until the Red Sea crossing. This occasion is the first in which God appears specifically as a warrior.

Nonetheless, the theme is implicit in texts that reflect even earlier periods of redemptive history. Indeed, a struggle erupts in Genesis 3, the story of the Fall.

Before the Fall, Adam and Eve existed in a perfect three-way harmony. There was an intimate relationship between the human couple and God, and also between Adam and Eve. The appearance of the serpent disturbed the harmony of the garden and resulted in complete disruption in both divine and human relationships. The conflict is most closely described in the context of the divine curse, particularly the curse against the serpent:

> Cursed are you above all the livestock
> and all the wild animals!
> You will crawl on your belly
> and you will eat dust
> all the days of your life.
> And I will put enmity
> between you and the woman,
> and between your offspring and hers;
> he will crush your head,
> and you will strike his heel. (Ge 3:14–15)

Debates rage about the interpretation of this pivotal passage.[1] For our purpose, we are most interested in exploring the nature of the serpent. On the principle that Scripture interprets Scripture (a traditional formulation of what is today called the canonical approach), it is legitimate to ask if anywhere else the Bible addresses this question. The New Testament, we discover, identifies the serpent with Satan, God's most potent enemy, in a passage that details the final outcome of the conflict first addressed in Genesis 3:15:

> And there was war in heaven. Michael and his angels
> fought against the dragon, and the dragon and his angels
> fought back. But he was not strong enough, and they lost

---

[1]See G. Van Groningen, *Messianic Revelation in the Old Testament* (Grand Rapids: Baker, 1990), 75, 79–80, 107–8, 110.

their place in heaven. The great dragon was hurled down—
that ancient serpent called the devil, or Satan, who leads
the whole world astray. He was hurled to the earth, and
his angels with him. (Rev 12:7–9; cf. Ro 16:20)

The New Testament speaks explicitly and frequently of
the suprahistorical conflict between God and Satan (see the following chapters). The purpose of this present chapter is to
draw attention to the less well-known treatment of this theme
in the Old Testament. Space does not permit an exhaustive
study,[2] though it is unlikely that any of these authors would en-
dorse the approach taken in this book. We will serve our narrow purpose by studying passages related to one specific motif,
namely, God's conflict with the Sea. After all, as Wakeman has
suggested, the Sea is the "most general appellation of the monster in the Bible."[3] We will support this study with an examination of the pattern of divine warfare in the Bible and the ancient Near East.

THE DIVINE WARRIOR SUBDUES THE SEA

One of the most intriguing themes in the Bible is the conflict between Yahweh and the Sea with its monsters. The texts
that describe or allude to this struggle are almost exclusively
poetic passages of disputed date. Thus, we will not attempt a
chronological presentation. The scope of our study will allow
us to examine only a few of the major references.

Nahum 1:4a

He rebukes the sea and dries it up;
   he makes all the rivers run dry.

---

[2]See J. Day, *God's Conflict with the Dragon and the Sea* (Cambridge: Harvard
University Press, 1975); C. Kloos, *Yhwh's Combat with the Sea: A Canaanite Tradition in the Religion of Ancient Israel* (Leiden: Brill, 1986); and M. K. Wakeman,
God's Battle with the Monster: A Study in Biblical Imagery (Leiden: Brill, 1973).
   [3]Wakeman, *God's Battle with the Monster*, 190.

The context of this verse is Nahum 1:2–8, a divine-warrior hymn similar to those that are found in the psalms.[4] The previous verses describe God's anger and judgment, as well as his riding on the storm cloud chariot (v. 3).

Verses 4 and 5 describe the consequences of God's appearance as a warrior. The overall theme is that God causes nature to convulse at his appearance. Verse 4a appears at the head of the list and refers to devastation of the sea as well as the rivers. This word-pair ("sea/rivers") is a well-known one that may be explained by the broader Near Eastern background of this theme (see below). The verb "rebukes" (*gāʿar*) personifies the Sea and turns the conflict into a struggle between it and God. J. M. Kennedy persuasively argues for the translation "blast" rather than the weaker "rebuke" in this and other similar contexts.[5] The English verb "blast" is appropriate for the Hebrew verb, which has, according to Kennedy, "connotations of forceful and destructive movement of air, accompanied by loud, frightening noise."[6]

Psalm 18:14–15

He shot his arrows and scattered the enemies,
   great bolts of lightning and routed them.
The valleys of the sea were exposed
   and the foundations of the earth laid bare
at your rebuke, O LORD,
   at the blast of breath from your nostrils.

Psalm 18 shares this theme of God's struggle with the Sea, using the same verb ("rebuke/blast" *gāʿar*). This psalm is an

---

[4]T. Longman III, "The Form and Message of Nahum: Preaching from a Prophet of Doom," *RTJ* 1 (1985): 13–24; and "Nahum," in *The Minor Prophets: An Exegetical and Expository Commentary*, vol. 2. (Grand Rapids: Baker, 1993).

[5]J. M. Kennedy, "The Root g'r in the Light of Semantic Analysis," *JBL* 106 (1987): 47–64.

[6]Ibid., 59.

individual thanksgiving prayer. David describes how he called to the Lord in distress and God answered by appearing as divine warrior. It is interesting to note how here and elsewhere God's intervention is described as a victory over the waters of chaos.

Psalm 29:10

The LORD sits enthroned over the flood;
   the LORD is enthroned as King forever.

This psalm is one of the most frequently discussed psalms in recent years. Attention has been drawn to its close connection with the themes of ancient Canaanite religion.[7] The relationship is undeniable, though it is hardly necessary to suggest that the psalm was originally a Baal text in which a simple name change occurred.

The psalm calls on the congregation to worship God, who is pictured as a powerful storm. Verse 10 provides the climax, which praises God as a king whose throne is placed upon the flood waters. This theme calls to mind the Babylonian creation story, the *Enuma Elish*, which locates Ea's throne in the midst of the Apsu, the deep waters of the sea. The connection between God's kingship and the slaying of the Sea will be noted below.

Psalm 24:1–2

The earth is the LORD's, and everything in it,
   the world, and all who live in it;
for he founded it upon the seas
   and established it upon the waters.

---

[7]H. L. Ginsberg, "A Phoenician Hymn in the Psalter," in *XIX Congresso Internationale degli Orientalisti* (Rome, 1935); P. C. Craigie, "Psalm XXIX in the Hebrew Poetic Tradition," *VT* 22 (1972): 143–51; and F. M. Cross, "Notes on a Canaanite Psalm in the Old Testament," *BASOR* 117 (1950): 19–21.

This is one of a number of poetic contexts (see Ps 74 below) that connects God's creative activity with the Sea and/or its monsters. It is significant that these contexts are poetic, and that Genesis 1 and 2, if anything, distance themselves from any suggestion of creation by conquest. The poetic format, however, of the psalms allows for such a playful allusion to the mythological theme for polemical purposes. The subjugation of the waters theme is extensive in the Bible.[8]

Psalm 74:12–17

But you, O God, are my king from of old;
    you bring salvation upon the earth.
It was you who split open the sea by your power;
    you broke the heads of the monster in the waters.
It was you who crushed the heads of Leviathan
    and gave him as food to the creatures of the desert.
It was you who opened up springs and streams;
    you dried up the ever flowing rivers.
The day is yours and yours also the night;
    you established the sun and moon.
It was you who set all the boundaries of the earth;
    you made both summer and winter.

This passage is a confession of faith in the middle of a lament psalm. The psalmist pictures God as victorious in a struggle against a multi-headed sea monster named Leviathan. As we will observe in our discussion of the next passage, this monster is to be equated with the monster of the same name (*ltn*) in Ugaritic texts. In the same way as Baal destroys both Yam and Lotan according to Canaanite mythology, and in the same way as the creation of the world begins with the slaying of the sea monster Tiamat in the Mesopotamian *Enuma Elish*, so the psalmist relates God's creative activity to his annihilation of the sea monster.

---

[8]A. H. W. Curtis, "The 'Subjugation of the Waters' Motif in the Psalm: Imagery or Polemic?" *JSS* 23 (1978): 244–56.

Isaiah 27:1

In that day,
    the LORD will punish with his sword,
     his fierce, great and powerful sword,
Leviathan the gliding serpent,
    Leviathan the coiling serpent;
he will slay the monster of the sea.

The most striking feature of this verse is its closeness to the Ugaritic text *KTU* 1.5 I,1:

k tmḫs. ltn. bṯn. brḥ
tkly. bṯn. ʿqltn. (Rasur: s)
šlyṭ. d. šbʿt. rašm

When you killed Lotan, the gliding serpent,
finished off the coiling serpent,
the seven-headed monster ...

The similarity between the two passages illustrates in the most pointed way imaginable that the poets of the Old Testament drew on the conflict myths of the broader Near East to describe Yahweh's conflict with the forces of chaos.

Conclusion

The above passages represent a number of others that picture God in mortal combat with the monsters of the Sea. In discussing the pattern of divine war in the broader ancient Near Eastern context, we will observe a connection with the myths of Babylonia, Assyria, and Canaan. It is our contention that the imagery of God's war with the Sea reflects a cosmological conflict that is reflected in historical warfare but ultimately reaches its origins in the spiritual realm. The struggle finds its first biblical expression in the narrative of the Fall and finds more explicit statement in the New Testament, particularly in those texts concerned with matters of the end of time (Revelation).

COSMOLOGICAL SYMBOLISM
FOR HISTORICAL CONFLICT

A number of passages in the Old Testament use the language of cosmological conflict to describe conflict on the historical plane. One of the clearest examples of this phenomenon is found in Daniel 7, discussed at some length in the previous chapter.

The psalms often remember God's struggle at the Exodus in these terms. The parting of the Red Sea as well as the later parting of the Jordan River are described through the use of poetic personification as a conflict between God and the Sea:

Psalm 77:16–20

The waters saw you, O God,
    the waters saw you and writhed;
    the very depths were convulsed.
The clouds poured down water,
    the skies resounded with thunder;
    your arrows flashed back and forth.
Your thunder was heard in the whirlwind,
    your lightning lit up the world;
    the earth trembled and quaked.
Your path led through the sea,
    your way through the mighty waters,
    though your footprints were not seen.
You led your people like a flock
    by the hand of Moses and Aaron.

This psalm is a personal lament in which the psalmist suffers from an unspecified[9] grievance against God. He feels abandoned by God and, accordingly, has little hope. But the turning point comes in verse 10, where he remembers and recites God's past deeds. In the above-quoted passage, he

---

[9]For the lack of historical specificity in the Psalms, see T. Longman III, *How to Read the Psalms* (Downers Grove, Ill.: InterVarsity Press, 1988), 37–42.

specifically remembers the Exodus as a time when God saved his people who appeared to be in hopeless distress.

The psalm thus recalls a time when chaos (in the form of the Egyptian army) threatened God's people on the historical plane. It describes that life-threatening situation by using the imagery associated with cosmological chaos (the Sea). By comparing his present despair with Israel's trouble at the time of the Exodus, the psalmist experiences peace in the face of his personal chaos. After all, God had shown himself master of the forces of chaos at the time of the Exodus.

Psalm 114

When Israel came out of Egypt,
  the house of Jacob from a people of foreign tongue,
Judah became God's sanctuary,
  Israel his dominion.
The sea looked and fled,
  the Jordan turned back;
the mountains skipped like rams,
  the hills like lambs.
Why was it, O sea, that you fled,
  O Jordan, that you turned back,
you mountains, that you skipped like rams,
  you hills, like lambs?
Tremble, O earth, at the presence of the Lord,
  at the presence of the God of Jacob,
who turned the rock into a pool,
  the hard rock into springs of water.

A full analysis of the lively imagery offered in this psalm is not possible in this context.[10] We will pause, however, long enough to point out the interplay between historical event and mythological allusion.

---

[10]See S. A. Geller, "The Language of Imagery in Psalm 114," in *Lingering Over Words*, ed. T. Abusch, et al. (Winona Lake, Ind.: Eisenbrauns, 1990), 179–94.

The first stanza makes it clear that the events of the Exodus and Conquest are at issue here. The possession of Palestine is imaged as the creation of God's house or sanctuary. This theme fits in with the broader Near Eastern pattern of house building that follows victory over the forces of chaos (below).

These forces of chaos are the subject of the second stanza. Once again poetic personification serves the purpose of mythological allusion as the Red Sea and then the Jordan River are said to react in fear at the appearance of the divine warrior.

Daniel 10:12–14 and 10:20–11:1

Then he continued, "Do not be afraid, Daniel. Since the first day that you set your mind to gain understanding and to humble yourself before your God, your words were heard, and I have come in response to them. But the prince of the Persian kingdom resisted me twenty-two days. Then Michael, one of the chief princes, came to help me, because I was detained there with the king of Persia. Now I have come to explain to you what will happen to your people in the future, for the vision concerns a time yet to come."

So he said, "Do you know why I have come to you? Soon I will return to fight against the prince of Persia, and when I go, the prince of Greece will come; but first I will tell you what is written in the Book of Truth. (No one supports me against them except Michael, your prince. And in the first year of Darius the Mede, I took my stand to support and protect him.)

This passage is elusive in detail but hints at a struggle between heavenly powers that parallels earthly conflict. The exact identities of the characters are in some doubt. For instance, while Daniel's reaction to the one who touches him in verse 10 may indicate that the person is God, that identification is not certain.[11]

---

[11]J. E. Goldingay, *Daniel*, WBC (Waco, Tex.: Word, 1989).

What is clear is that all except Daniel are supernatural beings. The idea that different nations have their own supernatural protectors or representatives is not fully developed in Scripture (though see the Septuagint at Dt 32:8). Nonetheless, that is the case here, in this late biblical book. The evidence for this is the mention of the angel Michael as "your prince." as well as the fact that no earthly force could be imagined as providing the kind of opposition to God and his angels as that pictured in our passage. Though differing in detail, Goldingay[12] arrives at a similar conclusion in his analysis of this passage when he succinctly states that "the OT assumes that the results of battles on earth reflect the involvement of heaven," and also "heavenly powers share in shaping the events of earthly history."[13]

We also agree with Goldingay's conclusion[14] that Daniel is not presenting a picture of near equal good and evil forces. Daniel knows that God is all-powerful and that the ultimate victory is his alone, but that there is supernatural opposition of superhuman force is obvious, being implied in Genesis 3 and more fully developed in the New Testament.

SUMMARY

These few passages are to be understood only as illustrative of many others in which God's conflict with the forces of chaos on the suprahistorical plane are parallel with the conflict that occurs in human history.

---

[12]Ibid.
[13]Ibid., 312.
[14]Ibid., 312–14.

6

The Pattern of Divine Warfare in the Bible and the Ancient Near East

Both the *Enuma Elish* from Mesopotamia and the Baal text from Ugarit illustrate a basic pattern that is found in certain biblical texts. In this section we will first survey the pattern as it is found in the Near East and then the biblical materials for analogous patterns. Finally, we will evaluate and comment on the relationship between the biblical and the ancient Near Eastern materials.

THE NEAR EASTERN PATTERN

Near Eastern myths that narrate the conflict between a divine-warrior god and the forces of chaos share a similar pattern. This pattern has at least four and perhaps five different stages: warfare, victory, kingship, housebuilding, and celebration.

(1) Warfare

Jacobsen has argued that this instance is one of the few demonstrable cases in which the periphery may have influenced the Mesopotamian center.[1] Thus, we will begin each of these sections with a description of the Ugaritic text and then describe the Mesopotamian texts.

The conflict in the Baal text[2] is between Baal and Yam. It is with this war that the text (at least in its present fragmentary form) opens. Baal, with the help of the craftsman god, Kothar-wa-Hasis, fights the Sea (Yam) with his clubs.

The Mesopotamian myth of *Enuma Elish* actually narrates two conflicts with sea monsters. The first one describes the fight between Ea and the father-god Apsu. The second, which is the focus of the narrative, is the fight between Marduk and the mother-goddess, Tiamat. It is the latter conflict on which we will concentrate as we complete the description of the pattern.

(2) Victory

In all three of the above-mentioned cases, the outcome of the battle is victory for the divine-warrior god against the forces of chaos. Baal defeats Yam, while Ea and Marduk vanquish Apsu and Tiamat respectively.

(3) Kingship

All three victories are followed by some sort of coronation scene. Baal in effect becomes the leader of the pantheon, though scholars continue to debate the precise relationship between Baal and El.[3] As Marduk answers the call of the pantheon to save them from Taimat, the gods appoint him king over them:

---

[1]T. Jacobsen, "The Battle Between Marduk and Tiamat," *JAOS* 88 (1968): 104–8.

[2]KTU 1,1–10; a convenient English translation can be found in *ANET*, 129–142.

[3]F. M. Cross, *Canaanite Myth and Hebrew Epic* (Cambridge: Harvard University Press, 1973); and M. H. Pope, *El in the Ugaritic Texts*, VTS, vol. 2 (Leiden: Brill, 1955).

O Marduk, thou art indeed our avenger.
We have granted thee kingship over the universe entire.[4]

(4) Housebuilding

The fourth part of the pattern is clearest in the Baal narrative because it takes up so much of the narrative. After Baal defeats Yam, he receives El's permission to build his house on Mount Saphon. Much of the text concerns the building of the house by Kothar-wa-Hasis. Scholars have long believed that this mythological building of a house for the god reflects the building of the god's actual temple.

(5) Celebration

Once again the clearest example of this feature is found in the Baal text. Upon completion of the house, Baal throws a banquet to celebrate its completion and presumably his kingship.

BIBLICAL ANALOGUES TO THE MYTHIC PATTERN

We will here present three examples of the pattern in the biblical material, two from the Old Testament and one from the New. This is not exhaustive,[5] but rather representative. The first Old Testament example is from a specific poetical text, while the second is a broader pattern embedded in Israel's early history and recorded in the narrative.

Exodus 15

In this case, the fifth element of celebration is part of the text itself. In other words, Exodus 15:1–18, the so-called Song of

---

[4] *ANET*, 66a.
[5] W. R. Millar, *Isaiah 24–27 and the Origin of Apocalyptic*, HSM, vol. 11 (Missoula, Mont.: Scholars, 1976), 24–27 presents a study of the pattern in Isaiah.

the Sea, is a psalm of praise for the victory that God won over the Egyptians. Thus, much of the poem describes the warfare (#1) and the resultant victory (#2). Reflection on God's power in warfare leads the psalmist to extol God's kingship (#3, v. 18) and anticipate the building of his house/temple in the land (#4, v. 17). This pattern has been noted in roughly similar form by Millar,[6] and before him by Cross[7] and Hanson.[8]

Israel's Early History

The basic pattern of war, victory, kingship, housebuilding, and celebration is reflected in the historical development of early Israel. The war is the Conquest, Israel's conflict with the Canaanite population that they encountered in the land. The divine warrior represented by the ark led his human army against the Canaanites who, because of their moral turpitude, stood in the place of the forces of chaos. The initial victories under Joshua were quick, but not conclusive. The cessation of hostilities did not occur until David subdued his enemies (2Sa 7:1). It is significant, then, that the issue of divine housebuilding was raised as soon as victory was achieved, though actual building was delayed until the era of warfare represented by David (a man who had "shed much blood," 1Ch 22:8) ended and Solomon ("a man of peace and rest," v. 9) came to the throne. Thus, Solomon built the temple at God's initiative, and when he did, he placed a huge laver of water before the temple that he provocatively called the "Sea" (1Ki 7:25–26). This name surely evoked the idea of the forces of chaos that God subdued in his warlike activity.

The concept of God's kingship was not new at the time of the Conquest or the building of the temple. Over against the

---

[6]Ibid., 83.

[7]Cross, *Canaanite Myth.*

[8]P. D. Hanson, *The Dawn of Apocalyptic* (Philadelphia: Fortress, 1975).

idea that God's kingship was a late concept or annually renewed stands the witness of Psalm 93:2:

> Your throne was established long ago;
>   you are from all eternity.

Indeed, the psalms that Mowinckel[9] identified as songs that celebrated Yahweh's annual enthronement are really divine-warrior songs that link God's kingship with his military victories.[10]

Revelation 20–22

One last example will anticipate discussion in the second
part of the book but will do so only with an eye on the pattern
described above. A number of contemporary scholars argue
that the book of Revelation has a seven-part structure.[11] Each
section gives a progressively fuller description of the final days.
Revelation 20–22 is the seventh and climactic vision and thus
gives the most detailed description of events that surround the
second coming of Christ.

The section begins with a metaphoric description of a
conflict that takes place on a supernatural plane. An angel
binds Satan and forcibly throws him into the Abyss. This victory over the prince of the evil kingdom is followed by a one-
thousand-year period, in which Christ is king. While there is no
hint of a banqueting scene in this final cycle, it is of interest to
note that the sixth cycle describes Christ's final victory (Rev
19:11–16), followed by a gruesome victory banquet in which
carrion birds feast on the corpses of the defeated army.

After a one-thousand-year period is a second conflict (Rev
20). An intra-evangelical debate has raged during the last century and a half over the significance of this chapter. The two
schools have been called premillennialism and amillennialism.

---

[9]S. Mowinckel, *He That Cometh* (Oxford: Basil Blackwell, 1956).

[10]T. Longman III, "Psalm 98: A Divine Warrior Victory Song," *JETS* 27
(1984): 267–74.

[11]A. Hoekema, *The Bible and the Future* (Grand Rapids: Eerdmans, 1979).

The view represented in this book is most closely related to the latter.[12] The most likely interpretation is that the initial conflict (20:1–3) is associated with Christ's victory over Satan on the cross, while the second conflict (20:7–15) is associated with the second coming at the end of the ages.

Once again, conflict and victory are followed by a royal motif (Rev 20:11), but even more interesting is the mention of the temple building theme in the context of the description of the New Jerusalem. That the vision includes a statement that there is an absence of the temple in the New Jerusalem is significant in that the narrator feels compelled to mention it at all: "I did not see a temple in the city, because the Lord Almighty and the Lamb are its temple" (21:22). No temple is needed because the new Jerusalem is like the garden of Eden. God is present everywhere. There is no need for a special holy place. Indeed, much of the imagery leads the reader to believe that the New Jerusalem supersedes the glory of the garden of Eden (22:2).

CONCLUSION

This chapter serves two broad purposes. The first is to provide evidence that the Old Testament knows of a cosmological/supernatural conflict in addition to and integrally connected with holy war on the human plane. This warfare becomes a major theme of the theologically more developed New Testament.

The second purpose of the chapter describes two divine-warrior myths from the broader Near East at whose heart is the same conflict between the gods of order and the forces of chaos. In the Bible as well as in the *Enuma Elish* and the Ugaritic Baal and Anat text, the forces of evil are related to the water/sea imagery and often follow a similar pattern of development.

---

[12]T. Longman III, "What I Mean by Historical-Grammatical Exegesis—Why I am Not a Literalist," *GTJ* 11 (1990): 137–55.

PART 2

The New Testament

PART 2

The New Testament

7

Jesus: New Exodus, New Conquest

Historically speaking, the divine warrior motif was inherited by the New Testament writers both through the Old Testament and through post-biblical Jewish reflection and writings. Since this study focuses primarily on the canonical texts of the Christian Bible, we will skip over the years intervening the two Testaments. But we will occasionally refer to the texts from this era to elucidate the New Testament.

We must also acknowledge that, historically speaking, the Gospels are not the earliest documents of the New Testament. From a canonical perspective, however, they provide a logical starting point in introducing us to the ministry of Jesus and to the evangelists' perspectives on the ways in which God the warrior was revealed in a new epoch of God's dealings with Israel and humankind in general. Here we narrow our focus to the three Synoptic Gospels—reluctantly, but in the interest of space—setting aside the opportunity of exploring the Fourth Gospel's development of the motif.

Each of the Synoptic Gospels utilizes elements of the divine warrior tradition, but two basic dimensions of conflict and triumph emerge: the conflict between Jesus and demonic powers, and the future return of the Son of Man on the clouds of heaven. We will concentrate on Mark's use of the motif, primarily focusing on key episodes in his Gospel and breaking away occasionally to consider Matthew and Luke. As we will see, Mark weaves into his narrative a remarkable number of allusions to the divine warrior tradition, primarily refracted through Isaiah's depiction of a coming New Exodus.[1]

OVERTURE TO BATTLE

Mark's echoes of Old Testament texts are redolent with the anticipation of a New Exodus. The blend of Exodus 23:20, Malachi 3:1, and Isaiah 40:3 suggests the motif of a procession in the desert through which the divine warrior will march to his sacred mount, defeating his foes and establishing his sovereign rule. In the spirit of Israel's ancient traditions, we might look for the approach of the ark of the covenant accompanied by the countless thousands of Yahweh's people, or of a violent storm blowing up from Seir in the south. But Mark focuses our attention on first one and then a second individual fulfilling a divine mission in the desert. And the allusion to Malachi 3:1 carries with it the possibility that Yahweh will come in judgment, for the fragment of verse Mark cites from the prophet continues in Malachi, "then suddenly the Lord ... will come to his temple.... But who can endure the day of his coming" (Mal 3:1b–2; cf. 4:5–6; Mk 9:12–17). Mark's prologue is an overture to his Gospel, establishing the theme of Israel's new beginnings.[2]

---

[1]Here we recognize our indebtedness to R. E. Watts, *The Influence of the Isaianic New Exodus on the Gospel of Mark* (Ph.D. diss., University of Cambridge, 1990), which at many points has corroborated our observations and at others helped to advance our thesis. The broad contours and several details of our reading of Mark have also been substantiated by W. M. Swartley, *Israel's Scripture Traditions and the Synoptic Gospels: Story Shaping Story* (Peabody, Mass.: Hendrickson, 1994), and J. Marcus, *The Way of the Lord: Christological Exegesis of the Old Testament in the Gospel of Mark* (Louisville: Westminster/John Knox, 1992).

[2]Although the association of desert with testing, murmuring, and disobedience is common in the OT, Second Temple Judaism had a strong tradition of regarding the desert in positive terms established by texts such as Isa 35:1–2; 40:3–5; 63:11–14; Eze 20:33–44; Hos 2:14–23. Qumran seems to

The herald of this story is not the angel of the Lord who prepared the way for Israel in the desert, but a prophetic figure styled after Elijah (Mk 9:11–13; cf. Mt 11:14). John's dress, as Mark describes it, is unmistakable. Elijah himself was centrally related to holy warfare in his day, most plainly in his dramatic assumption into heaven by fiery chariot (2Ki 2:11–12).[3] Moreover, he was prophesied to reappear before the coming of the "great and terrible day of the LORD" (Mal 4:5–6 [MT 3:23–24]; cf. Sir 48:10).

So now, at the Jordan, on the edge of Israel's holy space (cf. m. Kel 1:6–9), a prophetic figure readies God's people for the approach of the divine warrior by immersing the faithful repentants in the very waters that parted for Israel's original entry into the land. John does not go to Jerusalem, but calls Israel out to the ancient place of testing, judgment, and new beginnings. There he speaks of "one more powerful than I" who will come (Mk 1:7), suggesting a warrior figure who will initiate an epochal event in redemptive history. This one will bring the baptism, or deluge, of the Spirit, a feature suggesting God's outpouring of judgment and salvation in the last day.[4]

THE WARRIOR ANOINTED

Jesus arrives at the Jordan, and his baptism by John is accompanied by the descent of the Spirit. By submitting to baptism, Jesus identifies himself with repentant Israel and its

---

have been settled by Jews who maintained the Isaianic hope of a New Exodus (cf. Isa 40:3–4; 1QS 8:12–16). Josephus describes first-century movements that rallied in the desert under the leadership of Theudas (*Ant* 20 §§97–99), the Egyptian (*Ant* 20 §§168–72; *J.W.* 2 §§261–63), and a certain unnamed prophet (*Ant* 20 §188). See Barnett, "The Jewish Sign Prophets–A.D. 40–70: Their Intentions and Origin," *NTS* 27 (1981): 679–97.

[3]M. Lind, *Yahweh is a Warrior* (Scottdale, Pa.: Herald, 1980), 135, 140.

[4]For the background for this Spirit imagery see Isa 4:4 and its messianic application in Isa 11:1–4; 1En 49:2–3; 62:1–2; PS 17:37; 18:7. "Spirit and fire," found in Mt 3:11 and Lk 3:16, suggests that Mark's mention of only the "spirit" carries this dramatic connotation of eschatological judgment (applied to a messianic figure in 4Ezr 13:8–11).

preparation for the New Exodus and Conquest[5] (and, in light of the end of the story, we see one who will endure the wrath of God as he ransoms the many). The parting of the heavens and the descent of the Spirit may recall the plea of Isaiah 64:1, that God might rend the heavens and descend in his glorious conquering power as he had in days of old. In the days of Moses (Isa 63:11–12), the Lord had sent his Holy Spirit, closely associated with Yahweh's "glorious arm of power," to guide his servant and Israel to victory. So now, in the dawning of a new day of Exodus, the Spirit descends on Jesus and fits him for holy warfare.

The significance of the event is made clear by the voice from heaven declaring, "You are my Son, whom I love; with you I am well pleased" (Mk 1:11). As Son, Jesus is identified as the representative of the true Israel, whose divine sonship was defined in the desert (Ex 4:22; Hos 1:1; cf. also Isaac in Ge 22:12) and particularly focused in her royal Davidic king (Ps 2:7). As object of God's pleasure, Jesus is described as the Isaianic Servant in whom God will delight (Isa 42:1) and whom he will invest with his Spirit in order that he might bring forth justice (Isa 42:1, 3; cf. the hymn of praise to the divine warrior that follows in Isa 42:10–13). Both of these implied ascriptions, Son and Servant, carry with them remembrances of the divine warrior tradition: The Davidic son, to whom Yahweh grants victory,[6] and the Servant of Yahweh, who, through his suffering, will emerge exalted and triumphant (Isa 52:13; 53:12).[7]

---

[5]U. Mauser, *Christ in the Wilderness,* SBT 21 (Naperville, Ill.: Allenson, 1957), 24.

[6]At least one scroll from Qumran (4QFlor 1:10–11 [4Q174]) interprets Psalm 2 in terms of eschatological conflict, with the enraged nations arrayed around the Lord and his Messiah seen as the forces of Belial set against the elect of Israel.

[7]For a Jewish interpretation of the Servant of Yahweh as victorious Messiah, see the Targum on Isaiah 53. This understanding may also be implied in 1 Enoch's ascription of servant-like characteristics to the Son of Man figure as, e.g., the "Elect One" (1En 48:4–6; 62:1; cf. Isa 42:6; 49:2–7; 60:10; 61:1–2) and "the light to the Gentiles" (1En 48:4; cf. Isa 42:6; 49:6).

Matthew and Luke also describe the Baptist as one who fulfills the words of Isaiah the prophet as he prepares the way for the coming of the Lord. Luke continues the quotation from Isaiah 40:3, citing verses 4–5, which speak of the leveling of the mountains and valleys and the creation of a straight and smooth highway.

Both Matthew and Luke note that John comes preaching a prophetic message of repentance and forgiveness, barbed with a note of impending judgment. While John baptizes with water, following him will come one more powerful than he who will bring the eschatological deluge of spirit and fire.[8] The eschatological message of John is further seen in Matthew and Luke, where John the Baptist speaks of the coming wrath (Mt 3:7; Lk 3:7): the ax laid at the root, the unfruitful tree cast into the fire (Mt 3:10; Lk 3:9), and the chaff from the threshing floor consumed with unquenchable fire (Mt 3:12).

THE WARRIOR TESTED

Mark introduces Satan, the archenemy, in his thumbnail sketch of the temptation (Mk 1:12–13). The Spirit drives (*ekballō*) Jesus into the desert, where Satan tempts him for forty days, wild beasts accompany him, and angels come to his aid. Old Testament typology is clearly alive here, recalling Israel in the desert. Mark's previous use of New Exodus typology suggests that his temptation narrative, like that of Matthew and Luke, portrays Jesus as God's faithful Son who prevails over

---

[8]Cf. Joel 2:28–30; 1QS 4:21. For judgment with fire see Isa 29:6; 31:9; Eze 38:22; Am 7:4; Zep 1:18; 3:8; Mal 3:2; 4:1; Ps 5:6–7; 1En 90:24–27; 1QS 2:8; 4:13; 1QpHab 2:11–13. For imagery of fire as a flood, stream, or deluge, see the apocalyptic works of Da 7:10; 1QH 3:20–36; 1En 67:13; 4 Ezr 13:10–11. See also A. J. Mattill, Jr., *Luke and the Last Things* (Dillsboro, N.C.: Western North Carolina, 1979), 6–8 for his comments on what he calls the seven Lukan apocalypses of fire.

temptation where Israel failed.[9] Israel too was driven out of
Egypt into the desert (note *ekballō* in LXX Ex 12:33, 39), where
she spent forty years and was tested (Ex 15:25; 16:4; Dt 4:34;
8:2) before marching into the land and driving out its occupants.

The Matthean and Lukan accounts of the temptation are
notably more complete than Mark's, with three incidents in
which Satan repeatedly tempts Jesus in his capacity as Son of
God. In each challenge–turning stone to bread, trusting in
miraculous deliverance by angels, worshiping Satan in ex-
change for world sovereignty–Jesus answers with words from
Deuteronomy (Dt 8:3; 6:13, 16) and so proves himself the faithful Son who has been called and tested, and who will be re-
warded. Luke's placement of the temptation at the Jerusalem
temple as the last of the three probably reflects his own desire
to foreshadow Jerusalem as the final place of triumph, as well
as his noticeable emphasis on Jerusalem as the geographical
center of redemptive history (cf. Lk 9:31, 51, 53; 19:28). Luke
also accentuates the struggle between two kingdoms (Lk 4:6; cf.
Mt 4:9),[10] telling us that Jesus' initial triumph was marked by
Satan's strategic withdrawal "until an opportune time" (Lk
4:13).[11]

---

[9]But this typology could well include remembrances of Adam in Eden,
which even in its Genesis account seems to be rendered as a paradigm of
the experience of Israel. See G. Wenham, *Genesis 1–15*, WBC, vol. 1 (Waco,
Tex.: Word, 1987), 90–91.

[10]Susan R. Garrett, "Exodus from Bondage: Luke 9:31 and Acts 12:1–24,"
CBQ 52 (1990): 666, notes that the devil's blasphemous claim to sovereignty
anticipates his own demise modeled on the pattern of Isaiah 14:4–23 and
Ezekiel 28–32, passages recalled in Jesus' statement of Luke 10:18.

[11]Note Conzelmann's well-known view that Jesus' ministry is a "Satan-
free period," not to be challenged again by Satan until 22:3 (see H. Conzelmann, *The Theology of St. Luke* [New York: Harper, 1961], 28). Luke's use of
the perfect tense in Jesus' words to his disciples in 22:28, "you have continued (*diamemenēkotes*) with me in my trials (*peirasmois*)," will indicate that the
testings of the desert were an ongoing feature of his ministry. See R. P. Martin, "Salvation and Discipleship," in *Interpreting the Gospels*, ed. J. L. Mays
(Philadelphia: Fortress, 1981), 222.

Mark's peculiar mention that Jesus was "with the wild animals" is interesting to contemplate. Does it imply that Jesus, having withstood the testing of Satan, enjoyed his authority as New Adam over the created order (Ge 2:19–20; Isa 11:6–9; 65:25)?[12] Or are we to think of the desert as a place of curse (cf. Isa 13:21–22) and conflict (Ps 91:13), where wild animals and demons prowl (TIss 7:7; TNaph 8:4; TBen 5:2)? In any case, Jesus, at the outset of his ministry, faced the ancient enemy on his own ground.

The presence of angels completes the Markan picture of Jesus in eschatological conflict and deserves notice. In the biblical story we read of the angel of the Lord that led Israel through the desert (Ex 14:19; 23:20–23) and of an angelic warrior who reassured and strengthened Daniel after his vision concerning a "great war" (Da 10:1, 12–21). The role of angels in aiding and strengthening faithful Israel in warfare was also applied to the Qumran War Scroll's script for eschatological battle (1QM 12:7–9; 17:5–8; cf. 2Mc 10:29–30). Thus, we should consider the possibility that the angels of Mark 1:13 are not simply emissaries of heavenly hospitality, but in their assistance (*diakoneō*) provide strategic counsel to Jesus the divine warrior at a crucial moment of eschatological warfare.[13] In the temptation, the warrior is tested in an initial ordeal, an encounter between the kingdom of God and the kingdom of Satan.

BATTLES WITH DEMONIC FORCES

Mark tells us that Jesus, having overcome his first encounter with Satan, proclaimed in Galilee, "The time has

---

[12]Judaism also symbolized the nations as animals over which Israel, or its representative, would rule as Adam did over the creatures of the garden (Da 7; Ps 74:19; 1En 89:10–27).

[13]Cf. the role of the angel in Luke's Gethsemane account (Lk 22:43). The role of angels in God's eschatological warfare is clear enough, but it is interesting to note the Jewish tradition that fallen angels were originally responsible for instructing humans in the art of warfare (1En 8:1; 69:6).

come.... The kingdom of God is near. Repent and believe the good news!" (1:15). With these summary words, Mark makes a transition from his prologue to his account of Jesus, the eschatological deliverer, who will confront men and women with the nearness of the kingdom of God (cf. Isa 52:7; 61:1). Implied in this Gospel is the imminent victory of God over the demonic forces ruling this age.[14]

The ongoing nature of Jesus' battle with demonic forces will become evident in the first nine chapters of Mark, in the recurring accounts of Jesus' driving out demons. The first such account (1:23–28) lies at the opening of his ministry. In a synagogue at Capernaum Jesus encounters a man possessed by an "unclean spirit" (*anthropōs en pneumati akathartō*). The demon cries out, "What do you want with us, Jesus of Nazareth? Have you come to destroy us? I know who you are—the Holy One of God!" (1:24).

The question of the demon in verse 24—which may just as well be read as an exclamation ("You have come to destroy us!")—accentuates the warlike mission of Jesus against the demonic world. The recognition by the demon of Jesus' identity, "the Holy One of God," is probably an attempt on the part of the demon to overpower Jesus, premised on the ancient idea that to know a person's name is to know his or her identity and so gain power over the person.[15] "Holy One of God" was not a Jewish messianic title (used elsewhere of Jesus in the New Testament only in the parallel passage, Lk 4:34, and in Jn 6:69 on the lips of Peter) and could possibly indicate only a recognition

---

[14]For an eschatological messenger who proclaims in Isaianic terms the good news of the eschatological work of Yahweh, including the defeat of evil spirits, see 11QMelch. The LXX Ps 95:5, in the context of calling Israel to proclaim (*euangelizomai*) Yahweh's salvation (95:2), declares that all the gods of the nations are demons (*hoti pantes hoi theoi tōn ethnōn daimonia*).

[15]See among others, J. M. Hull, *Hellenistic Magic and the Synoptic Tradition*, SBT, vol. 28 (Naperville, Ill.: Allenson, 1974), 61–71; G. Twelftree, *Christ Triumphant* (London: Hodder & Stoughton, 1985), 39–54, 60–66.

of Jesus' close relationship with God.[16] Indeed, the ascription bears similarity to "Son of God," a title that the demons commonly used to address Jesus (Mk 3:11; cf. 5:7) and about which they were instructed to keep silent (Mk 3:12; cf. 1:34).

But could it also imply a recognition of Jesus as a mighty sanctified warrior?[17] Mark tells us that the Holy One of God is set against "an evil spirit,"[18] who recognizes the threat of imminent destruction ("destroy," *apollymi*), a word reminiscent of the *ḥerem* of Yahweh's warfare. The irony is that this initial engagement takes place in one of Israel's synagogues—an event that may foreshadow a peaking of the conflict in Jesus' later action in another place of worship, Jerusalem's temple. Mark seems to be portraying Jesus as the true restorer of Israel, the divine warrior reconquering holy space.[19]

This reading of the text is reinforced by Jesus' *rebuke* (*epitimaō*) of the demon, a word that particularly bears on our theme. Although it consistently appears in the narrative framework of Mark (and is frequently adopted by Luke[20]), the use of *epitimaō* coheres with what we find in the sayings and deeds of Jesus and strongly suggests an awareness of the Semitic

---

[16]Twelftree, *Christ Triumphant*, 62.

[17]Cf. Aaron in Ps 106:16; Elisha in 2Ki 4:9; Samson in Jdg. 16:17; Moses in Sir 45:2 (cf. WS 11:1–3). See R. A. Guelich, *Mark 1–8:26*, WBC, vol. 34A (Waco, Tex.: Word, 1989), 57.

[18]P. Pimental, "The 'unclean spirits' of St. Mark's Gospel," *ExpT* 99 (1988): 173–75, points out Mark's usual practice of first identifying the spirits as "evil spirits" (Mk 1:23; 5:2; 7:25; 9:25) and then referring to them as "demons." The decided Markan preference for the term "evil spirit" may be seen in its eleven occurrences in Mark, compared with Matthew's two and Luke's five.

[19]This campaign will climax in Jesus' symbolic destruction of the temple (for so Mark seems to portray it in 11:15–16), where the familiar *ekballō* will reappear (11:15), and the authorities, who show themselves to be on the side of the enemy, will resolve to destroy (*apollymi*) Jesus (11:18).

[20]Luke, following Mark, frequently uses the verb *epitimaō* (e.g., Lk 4:35 = Mk 1:25; Lk 4:41 = Mk 3:12; Lk 9:42 = Mk 9:25) to describe Jesus' commands directed toward demons.

equivalent of *epitimaō* and Jesus' understanding of his encounter with demons as divine warfare.

H. C. Kee has convincingly argued that behind this Greek word lies a term, the Hebrew *gāʿar* and Aramaic *geʿar*, which is frequently used as a word of command by which the enemies of God are overcome. *Epitimaō* is regularly used in the LXX to translate the Hebrew *gāʿar*. In chapter 5 we saw that this word may be translated as an explosive "blast," an instrument of Yahweh's wrath by which Yahweh defeats his enemies, including the Sea (Ps 18:15; LXX 17:16).

In prose accounts such as Zechariah 3:2, where the Lord is called on to rebuke Satan the accuser, the meaning shifts from an explosive blast to a powerful argument or authoritative word. Kee also points to the *Genesis Apocryphon* (1QApGen 20:28–29), where Abraham is said to drive out the evil spirit afflicting Pharaoh and his household (cf. also the use of *gāʿar* in 1QM 14.9–10). Kee probably goes beyond the evidence when he concludes that behind *epitimaō* lies a "technical term for the commanding word, uttered by God or by his spokesman, by which evil powers are brought into submission and the way is thereby prepared for the establishment of God's righteousness in the world."[21] Nevertheless, set within the Gospel story, this interpretive motif points us again to the broader redemptive archetype of Jesus as the divine warrior.

How do Mark's exorcism accounts compare with the other Synoptics? Luke's portrayal of Jesus' encounters with demons is far more like Mark's than like Matthew's. Luke, like Mark, depicts demons shouting and throwing their subjects about, while Matthew describes Jesus' encounters with demons in far less detail. They are, on the whole, orderly displays of Jesus' authoritative power.

---

[21]H. C. Kee, "The Terminology of Mark's Exorcism Stories," *NTS* 14 (1968): 235. See the critique of Kee's analysis by G. H. Twelftree, in *Jesus the Exorcist*, WUNT 2.54 (Tübingen: J. C. B. Mohr [Paul Siebeck], 1993), 44–46, who favors "expel" as a possible translation of *gāʿar*.

Luke's emphasis on the serious and pervasive nature of demonic activity is seen in the forty-four words (cf. twenty-three words in Matthew) of direct or reported demon speech,[22] as well as in their loud shouts and sudden outbursts (4:33; 8:28; 9:39) and in their physical abuse of their victims. The demons can overcome their subjects by their number (Lk 8:1–3; 8:29) and hold their subjects prisoners for many years (Lk 13:10–17).[23]

Luke retains the use of *epitimaō* in the exorcism accounts which he has taken over from Mark.[24] Luke, however, has Jesus rebuking the fever which overcame Peter's mother-in-law (4:39)—an element missing from Mark's account of the same incident (1:30–31). This is in concert with Luke's tendency to refer to deliverance from sickness and demons alike as "healings."[25]

On the one hand, this Lukan tendency may be explained by the understanding prevalent in the ancient world—that demons were the root cause of all sorts of human affliction (for evidence of Jewish belief, cf. Josephus *Ant.* 6.166, 168; 1QApGen 20; TSol 7:6; 18:20, 23). But it is also in keeping with the theme set in Jesus' Nazareth sermon, the jubilary release of captives in the favorable year of the Lord (Lk 4:18–19a = Isa. 61:1–2; 58:6). This Isaianic theme is itself related to the larger theme of New Exodus.[26] For both Isaiah and Luke, the

---

[22]J. M. Hull, *Hellenistic Magic*, 130.

[23]See J. B. Green, "Jesus and the Daughter of Abraham (Luke 13:10–17): Test Case for a Lucan Perspective on Jesus' Miracles," *CBQ* 51 (1989): 643–54.

[24]Lk 4:35 = Mk 1:25; 4:41 = Mk 3:12; and 9:42 = Mk 9:25.

[25]Cf., Lk 6:18; 7:21; and 8:2 Luke reports in summary the activity of Jesus, grouping diseases and demon possession together. In light of the rebuke of the fever in 4:39 and the case of the woman crippled by a spirit (bound by Satan for eighteen years) in 13:10–16, it appears that Luke wishes to extend the activity of Satan beyond demon possession into the broader field of sickness and disease.

[26]Note how the theme of Yahweh as healer is related to the Exodus experience in Ex 15:26.

release refers to all manner of bondage, including imprisonment, sin, sickness, and death. And Luke's addition of demonic possession or oppression is true to the message of Isaiah, where we find the Exodus described as the divine warrior's triumph over cosmic as well as human adversaries (Isa 51:9–11). In a manner analogous to Mark, Luke uses this theme as an Old Testament *typos* for understanding Jesus and his ministry.[27]

The role of demons as enemies of Jesus finds its background in Judaism's perception that behind Israel's physical enemies lay malevolent spiritual forces.[28] Moreover, the idols of the nations came to be associated with demons. While this idea originates in the Hebrew Bible (Dt 32:17; Ps 106:37–38), early Judaism saw its development in the LXX (Ps 95:5; Isa 65:3, 11) and the Pseudepigrapha.[29] R. Watts has suggested that Mark, in his portrayal of Jesus' warfare against the evil spirits, has in mind the Isaianic picture of the downfall of the oppressing nations' idols, thereby signaling the time of Israel's deliverance.[30] This, as we shall see, is most clearly evident in the case of the Gerasene demoniac.

The possibility of the Markan associations with Old Testament holy warfare gains probability in light of the Sabbath controversy of Mark 2:23–28, where Jesus likens his own disciples' picking grain on the Sabbath to David and his men's eating consecrated bread. The story Jesus refers to (see 1Sa 21:1–6) implies that David and his men were fit to eat the bread (in their case the Sabbath was not the issue) because they

---

[27]See S. R. Garrett, "Exodus from Bondage: Luke 9:31 and Acts 12:1–24," 656–80.

[28]E.g., 1QS 4; 1QM passim; 11QMelch 4–6; 1 En 54:4–5; TLevi 18:12; TZeb 9:8; TSim 6:6; TDan 5:10–13.

[29]Cf. Jub 1:11; 11:4; 22:17; 1 En 19:1; 99:7; 1 Cor 10:20; Rev 9:20. See Foerster, *TDNT* 2.10–16; G. Theissen, *The Miracle Stories of the Early Christian Tradition* (Philadelphia: Fortress, 1983), 255–56.

[30]R. Watts, *Isaianic New Exodus*, chap. 5.

were consecrated for war.[31] This may also be implied for Jesus and his disciples, who are even more qualified because of their eschatological mission of warfare under the leadership of the Son of Man. The saying about the Sabbath being made for man and not man for the Sabbath (Mk 2:27) might then be seen in a new light, with "man" referring not to humanity in general (as it is usually understood), but to Israel in particular, for whom the Sabbath was created (Jub 2:30–31).[32] Now, in the moment of eschatological crisis, the pertinence of this principle comes into sharp focus. The Twelve and the Son of Man are on a mission of divine warfare.

THE ARMY OF CHRIST

Mark informs us that whenever the evil spirits saw Jesus, "they fell down before him and cried out, 'You are the Son of God'" (Mk 3:11)–a submission and confession that underscores Jesus' success in his mission. As Mark has already implied, Jesus was not alone in his mission. He appointed the Twelve (vv. 14–15), and later sent them forth (6:6–7), to proclaim the kingdom and drive out demons. The Twelve symbolize the twelve tribes of Israel and represent a restorationist theme in Jesus' ministry. But it is frequently overlooked that within the context of the Exodus and Conquest, the twelve tribes could be regarded as twelve military divisions prepared for battle under the ultimate leadership of Yahweh, the divine warrior.[33] The role of the Twelve, as suggested in their

---

[31]So also M. J. Borg, *Conflict, Holiness and Politics in the Teachings of Jesus* (Lewiston, N.Y.: Edwin Mellen, 1984), 153–54, who recognizes the mission of holy war for David and his men, though he sees in Jesus and his disciples the analogy of a mission of urgency in which the future of Israel is at stake, not warfare per se.

[32]See ibid., 154–56.

[33]Note, for example, the military significance of the first and second census in Numbers 1 and 26, as well as the militaristic function of the twelve leaders of Israel in Numbers 13, who are sent on a reconnaissance mission.

appointment and sending by Jesus, appears to be an eschatological recapitulation of Israel's entry into the land. Even the theme of failure and resistance, which in Mark places the disciples on the side of the enemy, shows them to be akin to Israel in the desert and later in the land.

Luke also speaks of the sending of the Twelve (Lk 9:1–6), but his inclusion in 10:1–22 of the narrative of the sending and return of the seventy-two offers an intriguing contrast. The Twelve are sent on a mission throughout the villages. Characterized by austerity and singleness of purpose, they are charged with proclaiming the kingdom of God and healing. Those who do not receive the emissaries will be subjected to a symbolic testimony against them (9:5). No peace is offered.

Greater emphasis is laid on the account of the seventy-two, which even more clearly presents Jesus' followers as holy warriors–a *militia Christi*. The seventy-two are given authority to "trample on serpents and scorpions and to overcome all the power of the enemy." Their authority and protection ("nothing will harm you") clearly refer to the threat of satanic power. The power over serpents and scorpions is reminiscent of Psalm 91:13 (LXX 90:13), a psalm previously quoted by Satan in the temptation narrative and regarded within Judaism as a protection against demonic powers.[34] Serpents and scorpions as synonyms of demonic power seem to have been common currency in Jewish literature of the period.[35]

Several other features of Luke's narrative of the seventy-two suggest that Luke views the mission of the church from the perspective of divine warfare. (1) Jesus' response at the joyful return of the seventy-two, "I saw Satan fall like lightning from heaven" (Lk 10:18), is an unmistakable allusion to the heavenly rebel of Isaiah 14:12–20, the king of Babylon who "falls"

---

[34] See 11QPsAp a; 11QPs a; y. Erub 10:26c; y. Sabb 6:8b; b. Seb 15b.; cf. Josephus *Ant* 6 §168.

[35] See TSim 6:6; TLevi 18:12; TZeb 9:8. Within the NT see Rev 9:3, 10; 12:7–9; 20:2.

from his heavenly throne just as his earthly minions are "cast out" (*ekballō*) by the disciples. (2) The narrative of the seventy-two is set within the context of an allusion to Jesus as Elijah ("as the time approached for him to be taken up to heaven," Lk 9:51; cf. 2Ki 2:1, 11) and an apparent self-consciousness on the part of the disciples of embarking on a mission of Elijah-like holy warfare (e.g., the fire of Lk 9:54). (3) The role of the seventy-two, particularly in announcing the peace of salvation, the nearness of the kingdom, and their rejection as the occasion for a demonstration of the coming judgment of God, is remarkably similar to the Deuteronomic instruction for warfare against cities outside the land of inheritance (Dt 20:10–15).[36] (4) The demons submit (*hypotassetai*) before the name of Jesus as an accompaniment to the eschatological downfall of Satan. (5) The number seventy-two plausibly corresponds to the seventy elders (which may in turn intentionally correspond to the number of nations in Genesis 10, symbolizing Israel's mission to the Gentiles) who were appointed by Moses in the militaristic setting of Numbers 11 and were to assist Moses and receive a share of the Spirit that rested on him. (6) Jesus' warning that he sends them out "like lambs among wolves" (Lk 10:3) may draw on the Jewish tradition of referring to the nations as beasts (Da 7; cf. Ps 74:19), seen particularly in 1 Enoch 89:10–27, where Israel (numbered seventy in the biblical account)—the sheep—is brought by the Lord into the land of the wolves—Egypt (1En 89:14).[37] (7) The seventy-two as workers

---

[36]This raises the question of whether Luke implies that the Twelve are to be understood as enacting the conquest of the Land, which in Dt 20:10–15 precedes the instructions for total annihilation of towns within the land of inheritance (20:16–18). Cf. the role of the seventy-two with the parable of Lk 14:31–33, where a king, who is outnumbered by an enemy, will send a delegation to sue for peace.

[37]This strand of the Enoch literature is likely to have originated as early as the mid-second century B.C., and its apparent popularity among Jews may have provided a recognizable allusion to the Exodus complex of events.

in the harvest field allude to eschatological judgment,[38] in which the ripeness of the earth for harvest (whether of grapes or grain) recalls the memorable prophetic images of a harvest stained by the flow of blood like juice from grapes and the threshing of enemies like stalks in a field.

The effect of this evidence, taken as a whole or in part, forms a strong suggestion that the seventy-two are sent on an eschatological mission that is set in the context of divine warfare.

BINDING THE STRONG MAN

The Beelzebul controversy is a key passage in understanding divine warfare in the Synoptic tradition. Here the essential fact of Jesus' eschatological conflict is publicly unveiled. While the scribes of Jerusalem perceived that Jesus' conflict with demonic power lay at the heart of his activity, they misperceived the nature of the power under which he operated. For them he drove out demons by the power of Beelzebul, the prince of demons.

Here we need to step back from Mark and consider the meaning of this event in the ministry of Jesus and its place in the threefold Gospel tradition (Mk 3:22–27; Mt 12:24–29; Lk 11:15–22). The accusation that Jesus cast out demons by the power of Beelzebul seems to have implied that Jesus was a magician or sorcerer. For Jesus the accusation critically raised the issue of the source of his power and the focus of his work. His first strategy was to point out the absurdity of the accusation. It would be a self-defeating strategy for Beelzebul to cast out his own, just as it would be for any kingdom (*basileia*), city, or household to rise up against itself. The ultimate result of such folly would be its downfall. More to the point, if Satan's kingdom were divided against itself, Satan's kingdom would not stand (or as Mk 3:26 puts it with eschatological irony, "his end [*telos*] has come" NIV).

---

[38]Cf. Isa 27:12–13; 63:1–6; Joel 3:13.

Jesus' rhetorical question, "And if I cast out demons by Beelzebul, by whom do your sons cast them out?" implies a difference between his method of driving out demons and that of Jewish exorcists. Evidence of Jewish exorcists of the period suggests that many of them depended on techniques and mechanical aids similar to sorcery or magic. In contrast, Jesus' work of driving out demons, though employing certain techniques, appears to have been remarkable for its simplicity and authority. To his Jewish observers he would have been likened to a charismatic rabbi. His hallmark was a powerful word of command, never appealing to an outside authority to "bind" a demon. But Jesus did not develop this contrast in defending himself (it is probably only implied). Instead, he uniquely placed his emphasis on the eschatological context and meaning of his work.[39]

The key to the meaning of Jesus' exorcisms comes in an important saying found only in Matthew and Luke: "But if I drive out demons by the Spirit of God, then the kingdom of God has come upon you" (Mt 12:28; cf. Lk 11:20).[40] Three basic affirmations emerge: (1) God was at work as Jesus cast out demons; (2) the Gospel writers specifically attribute God's work in Jesus to the Spirit (or "finger") of God; and (3) God's work in Jesus is associated with the arrival of the kingdom of God.

These were bold claims, and they clearly set Jesus apart from Jewish exorcists. Indeed, of the critically accepted say-

---

[39]See G. H. Twelftree, *Jesus the Exorcist*, for a comparison between Jesus and his contemporary Jewish exorcists. Twelftree concludes that while Jesus' techniques would have been familiar to his observers, he was unique in connecting his exorcisms with the eschatological defeat of Satan in a cosmic, supernatural battle.

[40]The authenticity of this saying is reflected by J. D. G. Dunn's comment in *Jesus and the Spirit* (Philadelphia: Westminster, 1975), 44: "Indeed, if we cannot be sure that the Q saying preserved in Matt. 12.28/Luke 11.20 is a genuine saying of Jesus, we might as well give up all hope of rediscovering the historical Jesus, the man or his message."

ings of Jesus, it is one of our clearest indications that Jesus understood his encounters with demons as eschatological conflict. More pointedly, we will argue, these words imply that he viewed them not as exorcisms but as manifestations of the power of the divine warrior's operating in himself. Here is an important Christological affirmation.

It is significant that we never find the synonymous verbs *horkizō/exorkizō* ("to adjure, command, exorcise") or the noun *exorkistēs* ("exorcism"; cf. Ac 19:13) used of Jesus, though the demoniac in Mark 5:7 uses *horkizō* in an attempt to overpower Jesus by enlisting a higher authority. The terms were unquestionably a part of everyday Hellenistic vocabulary and were commonly used of Hellenistic and Jewish magicians. In this pericope and elsewhere, the word typically used of Jesus' work is *ekballō* ("cast out," "drive out"). In the LXX this Greek verb is used to translate the Hebrew verb *gāraš*. While this term can be used in numerous contexts, it is frequently and memorably used with reference to Israel, Yahweh, his angel, or the "hornet" driving out the Canaanites from the land of promise.[41]

As we have seen, the Conquest was an archetypal act of Yahweh, the divine warrior. If Jesus regarded himself as performing the eschatological work of the divine warrior, it would have been appropriate for him to refer to his encounters with demons in language derived from the Conquest tradition. The perception of Israel's traditional enemies as aligned with powerful spiritual forces is evident in Jewish apocalyptic thought (TDan 5:10–13; 11QMelch; cf. TZeb 9:8; TLevi 18:12), most notably in the War Scroll found at Qumran. There the faithful of Israel are aligned with the heavenly forces of light and set in

---

[41]Ex 23:28–31; 33:2; Dt 33:27; Jos 24:12, 18; Ps. 78[77]:55; 80[79]:8[9]. See Twelftree, *Christ Triumphant*, 105: "used mostly in the context where an enemy frustrating or standing in the way of God's fulfilling his purpose for his chosen people is 'cast out' so that God's purpose may be fulfilled." See also Twelftree, *Jesus the Exorcist*, 109–10.

opposition to the "sons of darkness" led by Belial—namely, the troops of Edom, Moab, Ammon, Philistia, and Kittim (1QM 1:1-2). This attempt to align nations and their rulers with personal spiritual powers was probably inspired by biblical texts such as Isaiah 24:21 and Daniel 10:10-14.[42]

But for Jesus, the enemy was perceived as highly individualized—demonic powers who exercised control over actual men and women within the borders of Israel (even more so than TDan 5:10-13). From an eschatological perspective, Jesus was carrying out a new Exodus and Conquest, routing the enemy that had occupied the land and held individuals in his thrall. God's reign could not be established apart from defeating the occupying forces. By binding the strong man and plundering his property, Jesus actually advanced the kingdom.

It was God's powerful Spirit or "finger" that worked this triumph. Matthew's reference to the "Spirit of God" directs us to think of Jesus along the analogy of prophets such as Elijah or Elisha, who performed mighty deeds in the power of the Spirit. Luke's reference to the "finger of God," whether or not it is original,[43] recalls the confession of the Egyptian magicians as they saw the plague of gnats induced by Moses through Aaron's rod: "This is the finger of God!" (Ex 8:19). Just as the Targums, or Aramaic paraphrases, are known to attribute acts of the Spirit in the Hebrew Bible to "the hand" of the Lord, so Luke may have used "finger" deliberately, thereby drawing a parallel between Jesus' work and the first Exodus—a parallel Luke knew to be true to Jesus' own understanding of his mis-

---

[42]See the discussion of principalities and powers in Paul below, in chap. 8.

[43]"Finger" is frequently argued to be the original wording of Jesus on the assumption that Luke, with his predilection for references to the Spirit, would have retained "Spirit" if he found it in his source rather than substitute "finger." But Luke's fondness for references to the Spirit may be overestimated. In the interest of developing his portrayal of Jesus as a prophet like Moses, he may very well have introduced this wording.

sion.[44] This would assist Luke in driving home the conclusion that Jesus was not practicing magic. Rather, his encounters with evil spirits signified a new Exodus, a fresh chapter in God's deliverance of his people.

Jesus' confession of operating in the power of an acknowledged agent of the dominion of God—the Spirit—would have made the essential nature of his work clearly evident. While Judaism did not associate the Spirit with exorcism, nor exorcisms with the establishment of the kingdom of God, it was believed that the Messiah would be empowered by the Spirit (Isa 11:1–4; PS 17:37; 18:7) and that the Lord, or one of his chosen agents, would deliver Israel from the power of the Evil One, Belial (TZeb 9:8; TDan 5:10–13; TLevi 18:12; 11QMelch). According to this saying of Jesus, it is God himself who is active in him, defeating the enemy. Moreover, the situation of victorious conflict with the powers of evil, joined with the arrival/presence of the kingdom of God, clearly suggests that Jesus was operating as, or in the power of, the divine warrior.

This line of interpretation is further strengthened by the parabolic saying regarding the binding of the strong man (Mk 3:27; Mt 12:29; Lk 11:21–23). Luke's wording differs from that of Mark and Matthew in some interesting ways (we will look at these later). But the basic picture is that of a strong man in his house guarding his possessions. How may someone enter and seize his property? He must first bind the strong man and then he can plunder his household. In the context of the Beelzebul controversy, the strong man takes on sinister features. Indeed, he can be none other than Beelzebul—Satan himself. Satan as the strong man controls property that he seems to have acquired by force and now guards by strength. He must be overcome.

---

[44]Note Luke 9:30, where the discussion among Jesus, Moses, and Elijah on the Mount of Transfiguration was about his "departure" (*exodus*), which he was about to fulfill at Jerusalem (see p. 119–21 in the next chapter).

More pointedly, the property is referred to as *ta skeuē* ("things," "vessels," or "instruments"). Used figuratively, this can refer to the human body as a vessel of the spirit. The picture might then be of Satan's controlling men and women by holding them captive in his "house"—or occupying them with his own spirits.[45]

More so than Matthew or Mark, Luke presents the analogy of military force in the parable of the strong man. The "stronger one" is implied to be a warrior who conquers or "overpowers" (*nikaō*)[46]—rather than "binds"—the strong man who, fully armed (*kathōplismenos*), guards his own palace (*aulēn*) in order to ensure the safety (*eirēnē*) of his possessions. When the stronger one overcomes the strong, he takes the "armor" (*panoplia*) in which the strong man trusted and divides up the "spoils" (*skyla*).

This little parable develops the theme found in Isaiah 49:24–25, where Yahweh, "the Mighty One of Jacob" (v. 26), vows to overcome Israel's foes, taking plunder from warriors and rescuing captives from the fierce:

> Can plunder be taken from warriors,
>   or captives rescued from the fierce?
> But this is what the LORD says:
> "Yes, captives will be taken from warriors,
>   and plunder retrieved from the fierce;
> I will contend with those who contend with you,
>   and your children I will save."

In the Old Testament, "The Mighty One of Jacob" (cf. Ge 49:24; Ps 132:2; Isa 1:24; 10:34; 60:16) is an epithet of the divine warrior. It finds an intriguing correlation in our passage,

---

[45]See BAG, 761, which cites e.g., TNaph 8:6, *ho diabolos oikeioutai auton hōs idiōn skeuos*; "the devil will inhabit him [the one who does not do the good] as his own instrument." The idea of Beliar holding as captives those who will be liberated is present in TZeb 9:8 and TDan 5:11, though the possibility that these are Christian interpolations cannot be excluded.

[46]This is the only occurrence of *nikaō* ("to conquer") in the Synoptics (cf. Jn 16:33).

where the reference to the "strong" one and the "stronger" one (albeit only in Lk 11:22) also recalls John the Baptist's announcement that the "more powerful" one would follow him, whose ministry (specifically "baptism") would be accompanied by the power of the Spirit (Mk 1:7–8; cf. Mt 3:11–12; Lk 3:16). Thus, seen from the perspective of the Old Testament, Jesus refers to himself as the "Mighty One" who is now bringing deliverance. Luke, in the *Magnificat*, has already drawn our attention to the renewed activity of the "Mighty One" (*ho dynatos*) who has performed mighty deeds with his arm, brought down rulers from their thrones, and shown mercy to his servant Israel (Lk 1:49–55).

It should be noted that Isaiah 49:24–25 lies between two Servant passages (Isa 49:1–6; 50:4–9). Moreover, the motif of *plunder* and the *strong* (if not the precise vocabulary) reappears in the Suffering Servant passage of Isaiah 52:13–53:12: "Therefore I will give him a portion among the great, and he will divide the spoils with the strong, because he poured out his life unto death, and was numbered with the transgressors" (Isa 53:12).[47] This final verse of the Servant passage seems to indicate that the Servant, having passed through a severe trial, is awarded as a mighty warrior a portion of the spoils of war. How might this fit Jesus' response in the Beelzebul controversy?

Interpreters of this parable have often asked, "When was Satan bound?" The wording in the Synoptics seems to imply that the binding was a past event (though Luke omits the phrase "unless first [*ean mē prōton*] he is bound"). It is frequently suggested that it took place at the outset of Jesus' ministry in his triumph over Satan's temptation. If so, the binding was only temporary and provisional, for Satan would be loose and

---

[47]See Susan R. Garrett, *The Demise of the Devil: Magic and the Demoniac in Luke's Writings* (Minneapolis: Augsburg Fortress, 1989), 45–46; J. Fitzmyer, *The Gospel According to Luke*, 2 vols., AB (Garden City, N.Y.: Doubleday, 1981–85), 923, finds the allusion possible in Luke.

active again as Jesus proceeded to his Passion. It might also be argued that the binding was a function of his ministry as a whole, just as his temptation epitomized an ongoing struggle which culminated in his Passion.

It is surely right to recognize the significance of Jesus' victory in his initial ordeal with Satan. The Synoptic writers agree on the importance of that event as a programmatic statement of Jesus' relationship with Satan and his kingdom. But perhaps we should read each instance of Jesus' driving out demons, healing, and preaching the gospel as a moment in which he plundered the palace of the strong man. Luke's Gospel suggests this in Jesus' vision, when the seventy-two returned, of Satan's fall from heaven (which precedes the Beelzebul controversy in Luke). But the echoes of the Isaianic Servant of Yahweh, which are present in Luke as they are in Mark and Matthew, may point to the death and vindication of Jesus as the epochal victory that enabled these plunderings. If we are correct in finding an allusion to Isaiah 53:12, that would serve as a reminder that Jesus' triumph over Satan was costly and painful from first to last.

Mark's version of the Beelzebul controversy lacks some of the militaristic details found in Luke and does not include the saying of the Spirit and kingdom, found in both Matthew and Luke. But the role of the Spirit is implied in the Markan warning against blaspheming the Spirit which, Mark informs us, was delivered "because they were saying, 'He has an evil spirit.'" This charge and Jesus' response find their closest Old Testament parallel in Isaiah 63:10, which recalls that Yahweh's deliverance of Israel at the first Exodus was met by rebellion that "grieved his Holy Spirit" and led him to turn, become their enemy, and fight against them.[48] Within the Markan context, the ominous possibility is introduced that the divine

---

[48]C. K. Barrett, *The Holy Spirit and the Gospel Tradition* (London: SPCK, 1970), 104–5; R. Watts, *Isaianic New Exodus*, chap. 5.

warrior's new work of deliverance might be met with an opposition that would provoke his wrath against Israel once again, thus recalling the latent threat of Malachi 3:1; 4:6 (Mk 1:2; 9:12–13).

CONQUERING SEA AND SUBDUING A LEGION

For Mark, the divine-warrior motif next surfaces in the episode of Jesus' rebuking the storm on Galilee (Mk 4:35–41) and, immediately following, in the story of the Gerasene demoniac (5:1–20). The storm, which threatened to capsize the boat and drown the disciples, recalls the archetypal enemy *Yam*, or Sea. As we have seen in our discussion of the Old Testament, Sea and River were regarded as cosmic enemies within the Baal myths, and Israel's sacred tradition portrayed the sea as a cosmic foe of Yahweh (Job 26:11; Ps 65:7; 74:13; 89:9–10; Isa 51:9–10; Hab 3:8, 15).

In light of Mark's use of the Isaianic new Exodus motif elsewhere in his Gospel and the echo of Isaiah 49:24–26 in the preceding Beelzebul pericope, we should be alert to the possible imprint of Isaiah in the story of Jesus' subduing the sea and the Gerasene demoniac. In Isaiah 51:9–10, the Exodus theme is mythically embroidered with the language of Yahweh subduing the sea and slaying the monster Rahab. Following shortly thereafter is the reminder that Israel need not live in terror of the oppressor, for Yahweh, the one who has power over the sea and the waves (51:15), will set the prisoners free (51:13–14). The juxtaposition of the stilling of the sea and the deliverance of the demoniac from an oppressive power gives further evidence that the evangelist depicts Jesus as the fulfillment of Isaiah's portrait of the divine warrior.

Mark tells us that the raging storm was threatening to destroy (*apollymi*) the boat and its occupants. As if to point out the correlation between this foe and the demonic forces facing Jesus, Mark employs the eschatologically loaded term *epitimaō*–Jesus "rebuked the wind." Moreover, like the divine warrior of old (Job 26:12; Ps 65:7; 89:9),[49] he commanded the waves to "be quiet" (*siōpa*) and "be muzzled" (*pephimōso*). Mark's use of *epitimaō* and *phimoō* in an identical manner in his first account of Jesus' driving out a demon (1:25) signals an underlying identity between these two phenomena. In each case Jesus, the divine warrior engages and conquers a cosmic foe.

The story of the Gerasene demoniac, the most detailed Gospel account of Jesus' engagement with an evil spirit, advances the theme of conflict and triumph. The destructive power of the evil spirit is evident in this strong man who dwells in the quintessentially unclean place—among the tombs. Once again the Markan correlation between demons and uncleanness comes into play. But here there is an added dimension in the situation; it recalls Isaiah 65:1–7, where apostate Israel is seen dwelling among tombs, keeping nightly vigil and eating the flesh of pigs (Isa 65:4; with LXX 65:3 referring to their burning incense to demons). The association between idol worship and sacrificial pigs in ancient Mediterranean religions is well known, and its Canaanite practice may have motivated the Pentateuchal prohibition against eating swine (Lev 11:7–8; Dt 14:8).

The hostile dimension of this supernatural force is underscored by the demon's name, "Legion." This name has puzzled interpreters because it suggests that the one is actually many.[50] But it is enough to note that Jesus is set against a hos-

---

[49]The universalism of Psalm 65 is particularly noteworthy, related as it is to Yahweh's stilling of the roaring sea. Psalm 89 clearly relates Yahweh's role as divine warrior (who, among other deeds, rules over the raging sea and crushes Rahab) to the establishment of the Davidic line and the crushing of his foes (vv. 21–23). Yahweh will set David's "hand over the sea, and his right hand over the rivers" (v. 25). Moreover, the theme of sonship is closely interwoven with this motif as David calls Yahweh "my Father" (v. 26).

[50]Cf. Jesus' reference in Mt 26:53 to the twelve legions of angels that he had at his disposal as he faced his arrest. In Roman military terminology a legion consisted of 5,000 or 6,000 foot soldiers and 120 horsemen. J. Jeremias, *Jesus' Promise to the Nations* (Naperville, Ill.: Allenson, 1958), 30–31n.5, suggests that "Legion" represents the Aramaic loan-word that could mean "soldier" as

tile force that is both vast and militant.[51] Moreover, the enemy recognizes the superior power of Jesus, causing the man to fall on his knees in obeisance, call Jesus "Son of the Most High God," and beg not to be tortured or sent out of the region.[52] Legion recognizes the threat of the approaching warrior–Jesus.

Against the background of idolatry and pigs, the otherwise curious sending of the idols/spirits into the herd of swine is a particularly fitting conclusion to Jesus' victory. It not only serves as evidence that the evil spirits have left the man, but within Mark's second Exodus typology, it recalls the drowning of Pharaoh, the god-king, in the sea (Ex 14:26–28; 15:3–5, 10; cf. Isa 43:16–17).[53] As in Exodus 15, the divine warrior exerts his sovereign power over both Pharaoh and the Sea. The spirits are banished to the watery corpse of a cosmic foe that Jesus has only recently subdued.

CONFLICT WITHIN AND WITHOUT

From this point through chapter 9, Mark relates the sending of the Twelve, who are particularly vested with authority over evil spirits (Mk 6:7) and enjoy success in their mission (6:12–13), and he tells of two more instances in which Jesus

---

well as "legion." The demon gave his name as "'Soldier, since we (the demons) are a great host (and resemble one another as soldiers do).'" The approximate number of two thousand swine that they then occupied represents the *telos* or "battalion" of infantry that numbered 2,048 (Josephus *J.W.* 1 §346; *Ant* 16 §469).

[51]J. D. M. Derrett, "Contributions to the Study of the Gerasene Demoniac," *JSNT* 3 (1979): 2–17, points out that *aposteilē* (Mk 5:10) can be taken as a military command or dispatch (e.g., Jth 6:3; 1 Mc 3:35), *agelē* (Mk 5:11, 13), can refer to a band of military recruits, *epitrepein* in the papyri and Xenophon is used in "issuing a military command," and *hōrmēsen* (Mk 5:13) could describe troops hastening to battle.

[52]In Lk 8:31 the point is more directly made when the demons plead not to be sent "into the Abyss."

[53]R. Watts, *Isaianic New Exodus*, chap. 5.

drives out demons. In the first instance, Jesus delivers the daughter of the Syro-Phoenician woman (7:24–30, performed from a distance); in the second, he drives out from a boy a demon of deafness and muteness, which the disciples were unable to expel (9:14–32). The explanation Jesus gives for their failure is that "this kind can come out only by prayer" (9:29).

As a whole, this story is exceptionally lengthy and detailed in its description of the violence dealt by the demon and seems to culminate a trend within the Gospel of an increasing ferocity in demonic resistance to Jesus.[54] Despite the disciples' previous victories in battle, they cannot continue self-assured.

Beyond this incident, we hear of the activity of an unnamed person whom the disciples have observed driving out demons in the name of Jesus (Mk 9:38–41). Jesus commands them not to hinder his miraculous works, "for whoever is not against us is for us" (Mk 9:40). It is as if in the day of eschatological battle the lines are clearly drawn. Anyone who engages the enemy in Jesus' name is an ally in the cause.

After Mark 9:38 and continuing on through the Passion narrative, there are no references to Jesus' or anyone else's carrying on combat with demons. But the theme of conflict does not disappear; rather, it is carried on between Jesus and the Jewish authorities and even with the disciples.[55] The parallels between the conflict with demons and with authorities may be observed in Mark's reference to the debates with Jewish authorities as "temptations." It appears that Mark uses *peirazō* as

---

[54]So W. L. Lane, *The Gospel according to Mark* (Grand Rapids: Eerdmans, 1974), 334–35.

[55]There are significant parallels between Jesus' conflict and victory over demons and his conflict and verbal victories over Jewish authorities. This is seen in the exorcism in the synagogue at Mk 1:23–28, with its hostile question and the authoritative word of Jesus. See J. M. Robinson, *The Problem of History in Mark*, SBT, 21 (Naperville, Ill.: Allenson, 1957), 44. See also A. J. Hultgren, *Jesus and His Adversaries* (Minneapolis: Augsburg, 1979).

a leitmotif to alert his readers to the ultimate source of the mounting conflict leading Jesus to the cross.[56]

But if the Jewish authorities oppose the kingdom of God and its purposes, the opposition of the disciples themselves becomes evident in their response to the Passion predictions. Beginning with Peter, who rebukes (*epitimaō*, Mk 8:32) Jesus and then himself is rebuked (*epitimaō*, 8:33) by Jesus and likened to Satan in his opposition ("Get behind me, Satan," 8:33), each of the subsequent Passion predictions is accompanied by behavior on the part of the disciples that sets them in opposition to the mission of Jesus. The epitome of their opposition is found in one disciple who betrays Jesus to the authorities (14:18–21, 43–44). Yet, Peter also falls away at the crucial hour of conflict, being unable, along with James and John, to resist Satan's temptation (14:38). At the moment of Jesus' arrest, the disciples desert him and flee (14:50).

With this theme of mounting conflict, we might expect Mark to highlight Jesus' role by employing the idiom of divine warfare. Indeed, certain key moments in the latter part of Mark seem to reflect this motif. We will examine these in the next chapter.

---

[56]Mark uses the verb *peirazō* only four times—once to refer to the temptation by Satan (1:13) and three times to refer to conflicts with authorities (8:11; 10:2; 12:15–16). The noun *peirasmos* occurs only at 14:38, where at Gethsemane the disciples are urged not to enter into temptation. The three temptations by the authorities in Mk 8:11; 10:2; 12:15 appear to be matched by three Passion predictions, each of which includes some reference to rejection, betrayal, or condemnation leading to death by the hands of the authorities.

8

Jesus: The Warrior Slain, the Warrior Triumphant

The approach and arrival of Jesus' final conflict in Jerusalem are marked by episodes in which the divine-warrior motif gives crisper definition to the significance of events. Here we focus on the Transfiguration, the Triumphal Entry, Jesus' apocalyptic teaching, and his death and resurrection.

THE DIVINE WARRIOR RESPLENDENT

The presence of the divine-warrior motif is suggested in Jesus' saying, prior to the Transfiguration, that some of those standing in his presence would not taste death until they saw the kingdom of God come with power (Mk 9:1). This may echo the Exodus story, in which only a few of the first desert generation lived to see the Promised Land.

The mountain ascended by Jesus and the three disciples is reminiscent of Sinai,[1] but the term for "high mountain" (*oros hypsēlon*) is also identical to that found in LXX Isaiah 40:9, where the herald of good tidings (recalling Mark's use of Isa 40:3 in Mk 1:3) is commanded to ascend a high mountain and proclaim to Judah, "Here [on this mountain] is your God!"–

---

[1]For a high mountain as a place of revelation cf. also Eze 40:2 and Rev 21:10. As a place of pseudo-revelation see Mt 4:8.

the Sovereign Lord who comes with strength and his arm with power (Isa 40:10 LXX). The imagery of the divine warrior's standing on a mountain is known in the Old Testament and elsewhere,[2] and the transformation of Jesus into a glorious figure accompanied by a cloud may be evoking this image.

The cloud that overshadowed Jesus on the Mount of Transfiguration is frequently compared to the cloud above the tabernacle that symbolized Yahweh's presence (LXX Ex 40:35 uses the same terms as Mark, *nephelē* and *episkiazō*) and led Israel on her march through the desert (Ex 40:36–38). Here again association with the divine warrior might intentionally resonate within the Markan context, in which the tone of the Gospel has been set by the theme of the prologue–the processional way through the desert (Mk 1:2–3).

The appearance of Moses and Elijah recalls their association with theophanies on Mount Sinai (Moses in Ex 24:12–18; Elijah in 1Ki 19) and with the divine warrior. Mark leaves the subject of their conversation with Jesus to the reader's imagination, though he may have thought he had provided enough clues. But Luke fills in the detail: they discussed Jesus' *exodus* (*tēn exodon autou*) "which he was about to bring to fulfillment at Jerusalem" (Lk 9:31), a theme that admirably complements Mark's new Exodus motif as well.

Finally, on the mountain, the heavenly voice once again affirms the Sonship of Jesus in terms reminiscent of Psalm 2:7 (Mk 9:7). From the first declaration of Jesus' Sonship at his baptism (1:11) to the use of the term by the demons (3:11) and now at his glorious manifestation, "Son of God" is closely related to Jesus' mission of divine conflict.[3]

---

[2]See Isa 31:4; Zec 14:4; cf. 2Es 13:35. Hittite and Syrian storm gods are depicted standing with each foot on a mountain. See M. S. Smith, *The Early History of God* (San Francisco: HarperSanFrancisco, 1990), 54, 73n.86.

[3]There is an additional parallel here between Jesus and Moses, both of whom descend the mountain and encounter failure in leaders and people: the disciples are unable to deal with a demon, and Aaron was unable to deal with idolatry (cf. Mk 9:19 with Ex 32:9; 34:9).

THE PROCESSION TO THE TEMPLE

Jesus is on "the way" to Jerusalem and the temple. And predictably, his Triumphal Entry and arrival at the Temple bear the imprint of the divine-warrior tradition. From the prologue, we know of Mark's interest in showing Jesus' fulfilling the hope of Yahweh's coming along the processional way to occupy Zion and his throne. When Mark cited his medley of Exodus 23:20, Malachi 3:1, and Isaiah 40:3, he was triggering a cavalcade of Old Testament associations. The force of this imagery can be seen in Isaiah 35, a passage we might expect to have special significance for Mark. There Yahweh comes triumphant (35:4) with his holy ones along the way, which has become a holy highway (35:8) that passes through the landscape of a new creation (35:6–7). Along this highway comes restored Israel—symbolized by the healed blind, deaf, lame, and mute (35:5–6)—returning to Zion with joy and singing (35:9–10).[4]

Mark develops the theme of the "way" in his Gospel,[5] repeating the term *hodos* sixteen times, seven of which occur between 8:22 and 11:1—a section appropriately called Mark's "Way" section.[6] Thus, the leitmotif of "way," established in the prologue by the echoes from Exodus, Isaiah, and Malachi, renders Jesus as the manifestation of Yahweh, the divine warrior

---

[4]Zechariah, another Markan favorite (see D. C. Allison, *The End of the Ages Has Come* [Philadelphia: Fortress, 1985], 33–36), can also apply this imagery both to the processional way of Zion's coming king (9:9) and to the triumphant arrival of the divine warrior, who seems to clear a highway (first for Israel's flight, 14:5, then for universal pilgrimage, 14:16) by splitting the Mount of Olives to form a valley (14:3–5).

[5]For the force of this theme in shaping the self-definition of the Qumran community, see 1QS 8:12–16; 9:17–20; 4Q176. Its influence may also be observed also in Bar 5:5–7; TMos 10:1–5; and PS 11.

[6]See W. H. Kelber, *Mark's Story of Jesus* (Philadelphia: Fortress, 1979), 43–56; E. Best, *Following Jesus: Discipleship in the Gospel of Mark*, JSNTSS, vol. 4 (Sheffield: JSOT, 1981), 15–145; J. Marcus, *Way of the Lord*, 12–47.

and king who is making his way to his holy mount and throne.[7]

It is no wonder, then, that the processional way of Jesus as the divine warrior takes him to Jericho (Mk 10:46) en route to Jerusalem. Once again, we are reminded of the divine warrior who has subdued his enemies and makes his way to his sanctuary. Accompanying him are the Twelve and–by literary license–a representative of the Isaianic restored Israel recently made whole, Bartimaeus (10:52).[8]

The culmination of this theme is in Jesus' Triumphal Entry into Jerusalem. Like the divine warrior celebrated in Israel's cultic hymns, Jesus' arrival is acclaimed by the crowds with lines from Psalm 118, a royal song of thanksgiving celebrating a military victory, in which Yahweh delivered the Davidic king from his enemies (Ps 118:7, 10–16). Used as a processional liturgy, it took the celebrants from outside to within the gates of the temple (vv. 19–20). In the mouths of the festal crowds surrounding Jesus, it signals the arrival of one who fulfills the hope for the coming of the Davidic kingdom (Mk 11:10, "Blessed is the coming kingdom of our father David!") and perhaps gives voice to Isaiah's rejoicing company of the redeemed (Isa 35:10). Jesus' own acknowledgment of his role in this eschatological drama is emphasized by his riding a colt, thus fulfilling Zechariah 9:9, in which the righteous and victo-

---

[7]See R. E. Watts, *Isaianic New Exodus*, chap. 4, for a thorough discussion of Mark's use of *hodos* as a clue to his structure. Watts (chap. 6) sees this section as part of Mark's Isaianic pattern and argues that Mark's portrayal of Jesus' healing the blind (at the beginning and end of the section)–as well as the blindness of the uncomprehending disciples–shows the fulfillment of the Isaianic Servant-Teacher, who opens blind eyes by teaching the way of Yahweh's wisdom.

[8]Note Mark's emphatic "And they came to Jericho." See Swartley, *Israel's Scripture Traditions*, 106, who also cites E. C. Hobbs' "The Gospel of Mark and the Exodus" (Ph.D. diss. University of Chicago, 1958), 47–48 and A. M. Farrer, *St. Matthew and St. Mark*, 2d ed. (Philadelphia: Westminster, 1966), 193–94. For a discussion of the healing of the blind as an Isaianic motif in Mark, see J. Marcus, *Way of the Lord*, 34–35.

rious Davidic king comes to Jerusalem on the colt of a donkey in order to assume his rule of peace.

But paradoxically, the divine warrior, having inspected the premises, finds the hour "already late" (Mk 11:11), and he withdraws with his band to Bethany on the Mount of Olives.[9] Jesus completes his procession along the way, entering the temple on the following day. This fulfills the latter half of Malachi 3:1 ("Then suddenly the Lord you are seeking will come to his temple"), the first half of which Mark alluded to in his prologue ("See, I will send my messenger ahead of you, who will prepare your way," Mk 1:2). Mark likens Jesus' arrival in the temple to the coming of the divine warrior. Just as Jesus has been driving out (*ekballō*) demons in the course of his campaign to retake land and people, so now he "drives out" (*ekballō*, 11:15) those carrying on commerce in the temple, thus symbolizing the wrath of Yahweh that is now directed against the disobedient within Israel's most holy space.[10]

Here again is a fulfillment of Malachi 3: "But who can endure the day of his coming?" (Mal 3:2). Moreover, the likening of the temple to a "den of [social] robbers" (*spēlaion lēstōn*, Mk 11:17) recalls Jeremiah's temple sermon (Jer 7:11) and the prophet's oracle of doom.[11] The incident also seems to parallel intentionally Jesus' first encounter with a demon (Mk 1:23–28). That episode also took place in a house of worship (a synagogue), where Jesus drove out a demon who recognized Jesus as one who came to destroy.

---

[9]There is surely more to Mark's comment than a reference to a time crunch in Jesus' itinerary! This is probably a comment on the spiritual state of Jerusalem and the temple.

[10]P. B. Duff, "The March of the Divine Warrior and the Advent of the Greco-Roman King: Mark's Account of Jesus' Entry into Jerusalem," *JBL* 111 (1992): 55–71.

[11]*Lēstēs* can refer to social bandits and revolutionaries, such as the Zealots. See G. W. Buchanan, "Mark 11, 15–19: Brigands in the Temple," *HUCA* 30 (1959): 169–77, and J. Marcus, *Way of the Lord*, 117. It is also possible that the "den of robbers" is meant to recall the house of the strong man in 3:27.

The judgment on Israel is doubly emphasized by Mark's framing the account with the cursing of the fig tree (Mk 11:12–14, 20–21). This again recalls the words of the prophet Malachi about the coming day of the Lord (Mal 4). Before "that great and dreadful day," Yahweh will send the prophet Elijah to bring reconciliation within Israel (Mal 4:5–6a [MT 3:23–24a]). But if that reconciliation does not come, Yahweh will come "and strike the land with a curse" (Mal 4:6b [MT 3:24b]). Earlier, Mark indicated by Jesus' saying about Elijah (Mk 9:12–13) that the prophet had come in the person of the Baptist—and had met his demise.[12] The cursing of the fig tree[13] reinforces the coming judgment on Israel, which (again appealing to Malachi) would be so complete that "not a root [Mk 11:20] or a branch [Mk 11:13] will be left to them" (Mal 4:1 [MT 3:19]).

THE COMING OF THE SON OF MAN

The Cloud Rider Rides Again

Against this background, Jesus uses the motif of the coming of the divine warrior[14] to speak of the approaching destruction of Jerusalem (Mk 13:5–23). The reference to the total

---

[12]Mark notes that Jesus began his proclamation of the kingdom *after* John was put in prison (Mk 1:14–15), thus consciously reflecting the pattern of Mal 4:5–6. We should also note that Jesus' response to the question of his authority to do "these things" (presumably his temple actions) is a counterquestion regarding the authority of John's baptism. The implication is that John operated under heaven's authority and that the religious authorities had not repented. Consequently, Jesus was now operating under heaven's authority to bring judgment against an unrepentant Israel. See R. Watts, *Isaianic New Exodus*, chap. 7.

[13]For the fig tree as a symbol of Israel or God's blessing on Israel, see Jer 8:13; 29:17; Hos 9:10; Joel 1:7; Mic 7:1–6. For its destruction as judgment against Israel, see Hos 2:12; 9:16; Lk 13:6–9 (cf. also Isa 34:4).

[14]Note the imagery of Mk 13:8: "Nation ... against nation, and kingdom against kingdom" (cf. Isa 19:2); earthquakes (cf. Jdg 5:4–5; Ps 18:7; 68:8; Isa 13:13; 24:19; 29:6; 64:1); famine (cf. Dt 32:24; Jer 15:2; Eze 5:17; 14:13); birth pangs (cf. Isa 13:8; 26:17; Jer 4:31; 6:24; 13:21; 22:23; Mic 4:9–10).

destruction of the temple with not one stone left on another (cf. Hag 2:15) clearly implies a second visitation of Yahweh in judgment against Jerusalem.

But while the destruction of Jerusalem and temple are implied to be Yahweh's judgment mediated through human armies, the coming of the Son of Man will be an event of apocalyptic power and glory and of salvation for the elect. A day of cosmic distress recalling the Day of the Lord (Mk 13:24–25), its central feature will be a recapitulation of the coming of the divine warrior who rode the chariot of the clouds as he came to deliver Israel in her times of distress.

Jesus speaks of the coming of the Danielic son of man.[15] In Daniel, the figure of the son of man conveys a penetrating perspective on the human predicament in which worldly kingdoms wage war against the saints of God (Da 7:21–22, 25), and spiritual powers preside over kingdoms and battle against the spiritual emissaries of God (10:12–14, 20). Whereas more ancient Israelite divine-warrior traditions understood Yahweh to be fighting against Israel's earthly enemies, the apocalyptic scenario deepened that perspective and unveiled the cosmic conflict lying behind the apparent ebb and flow of world empires, pointing to the final inauguration of the kingdom of God. The goal of Yahweh's conflict of the ages is the establishment of a universal and everlasting kingdom (7:14), and the real enemies transcend—or stand behind—the empires of the earth (7:2–8; 10:13, 20).

The imagery of the Son of Man as divine warrior was not lost on apocalypticists of the first century. Fourth Ezra 13, dating from the late first century A.D., describes "something like the figure of a man" who arises from the heart of the sea and flies "with the clouds of heaven" (4Ezr 13:3; 16, 36; cf., Da

---

[15]See I. H. Marshall, *The Origins of New Testament Christology,* rev. ed. (Downers Grove, Ill.: InterVarsity Press, 1991); B. Witherington, *The Christology of Jesus* (Minneapolis: Fortress, 1990) for the evidence that Jesus truly spoke of himself as the Danielic son of man.

2:34, 45). The author's elaboration on the theme of Daniel 7 is interesting enough in that it assigns messianic functions to a figure like the Son of Man. But more pertinent to our theme is the way in which 4 Ezra embroiders the role of the man-like figure with divine-warrior imagery. Everything under his gaze trembles; all who hear his voice melt as wax (4Ezr 13:4). Though he bears no spear or weapon of war, from his mouth comes a stream of fire; from his lips, flaming breath; from his tongue, a storm of sparks (13:9–10). Like the divine warrior, he delivers wind, fire, and storm (13:27). Even his standing atop Zion is an adaptation of the motif found in Zechariah 14:4, where Yahweh is described on the day of battle as standing atop the Mount of Olives. Accompanying these great acts of deliverance will be a new Exodus, as the Most High himself stops the channel of the Euphrates and leads back to Zion the ten tribes taken captive by the Assyrians.

The Convulsion of the Cosmos

Jesus' words regarding his future coming as the heavenly Son of Man also demonstrate an awareness of the divine-warrior tradition lying behind the title (Mt 24:29–31; Mk 13:24–27; Lk 21:25–28). The Synoptic Gospels agree that Jesus spoke of the coming of the Son of Man on or with the clouds (or "a cloud," Lk 21:27) in power and glory. This event would be preceded by a cosmic disturbance that is described in the traditional language of the coming of the divine warrior on the Day of the Lord. The sun and moon will be darkened, the stars will fall, and the "powers of/in heaven" will be shaken.

Luke diverges from Matthew and Mark, summarizing the cosmic disturbance as "signs in the sun, moon and stars" and adding a reference to the anguish and perplexity among the nations due to the roaring and tossing of the sea (Lk 21:25). The latter may recall the marine disturbance accompanying the emergence of Daniel's four beasts from the sea (note that 4Ezr 13:3 describes the Son of Man as also arising from the sea).

Matthew and Mark, on the other hand, speak of the darkness of the sun and moon and the falling of the stars. Their language echoes passages from Isaiah and Joel that describe events accompanying the appearance of the divine warrior on the Day of the Lord (Isa 13:10; 34:4; Joel 3:15–16 [= MT 4:15–16]). The reference to the shaking of the powers of heaven (found in all three Gospels) may draw on a cluster of biblical images associated with the execution of God's judgment against heavenly counterparts to earthly kingdoms.[16] In each of the Synoptics, Jesus speaks of the coming of the Son of Man as following immediately after these events, evocatively described in the language of the coming of the divine warrior.[17] Again, in Matthew 24:27 and Luke 17:24, Jesus likens the coming of the Son of Man to the lightning that flashes across the heavens.

Both Matthew and Mark explicitly locate Jesus' discourse on the Mount of Olives. There, *seated*, he speaks of the coming destruction of Jerusalem and the arrival of the Son of Man (Mt 24:3; Mk 13:3). The eschatological scenario is yet future; the time is not yet right for the divine warrior to plant his feet and *stand* atop the mountain (Zec 14:4; 4Ezr 13:35).[18]

---

[16]In Hag 2:6, 21, God will shake the heavens and earth and thereby overturn thrones and shatter the power of foreign kingdoms. In Isa 24:21, God will "in that day ... punish the powers in the heavens above and the kings on the earth below." Joel 2:10 speaks of the Day of the Lord when the sky "trembles," the earth "shakes," and the sun, moon, and stars "are darkened." Likewise in Joel 3:15–16, on the Day of the Lord the sun, moon, and stars "will be darkened," and when the Lord roars from Zion, heaven and earth "will tremble."

[17]Josephus, in his account of the Roman siege of Jerusalem (A.D. 69–70), reports a popular account that seems to have been shaped by the expectation of the coming of the divine warrior in judgment. On a certain day "before sunset throughout all parts of the country chariots were seen in the air and armed battalions hurtling through the clouds and encompassing the cities" (Josephus *J.W.* 6 §§297–99).

[18]J. Marcus, *The Way of the Lord*, 115–57, also recognizes the background of Zechariah 14:4 for Mark 13:3 as well as for Mark 14:26. The eschatological significance of the Mount of Olives seems also to have been recognized

The Son of Man Exalted and Coming with the Clouds

Finally, in the course of Jesus' trial before the Sanhedrin, the high priest asks, "Are you the Christ, the Son of the Blessed One?" Mark records Jesus' response as a combination of allusions to Daniel 7:13 and Psalm 110:1: "I am.... And you will see the Son of Man sitting at the right hand of the Mighty One and coming on the clouds of heaven" (Mk 14:62).

The significance of this saying for our understanding of Jesus as the divine warrior is found in the Son of Man "seated" and "coming." In a divine reversal of events, Jesus the victim will be vindicated and exalted to a position of regal glory and honor. And, as the echo of Psalm 110:1a implies, he will remain at the right hand until the Lord makes his enemies a footstool for his feet (Ps 110:1b).

By immediately following this echo of Psalm 110 with an allusion to Daniel 7:13, Jesus implies not only his fulfillment of the Davidic promise, but his future epiphany as the mysterious heavenly figure who would come to initiate the kingdom of God. Against the backdrop of Jesus' previous announcement of the coming of the Son of Man and the Day of the Lord, Mark 14:62 suggests an eschatological vindication characterized not only by judicial proceedings but also by divine warfare led by the cloud-riding Son of Man. The irony and arresting boldness of this declaration is that the high priest and elders of Israel, the very ones vested with the responsibility of guarding the traditions and holiness of the nation, would behold the coming of the Son of Man to seal their doom. The old theme of Yahweh the divine warrior coming to bring judgment against Israel is reborn.

---

by a certain Egyptian, a prophetic figure, who Josephus tells us appeared during the procuratorship of Felix (A.D. 52–60). Mustering a multitude of followers (Josephus reports 30,000), he promised to lead them through the desert to the Mount of Olives. There, at his command, the walls of Jerusalem would fall down, and they would enter the city (Josephus *J.W.* 2. §§261–263; *Ant.* 20 §§169–172).

APPROACHING THE CRUCIAL CONFLICT

We have already seen how Mark depicts Jesus' fighting a battle against demonic forces in league with Satan, as well as against Jewish authorities—and even against his disciples—who are shown to be opposing Jesus and the purposes of God. At one level of the narrative, it appears that this collusion between spiritual and human enemies, joined finally by the Romans, is the principal force leading Jesus to the cross. But Jesus' thrice-repeated predictions of his death and resurrection (Mk 8:31; 9:31; 10:33–34) under divine imperative (*dei*, 8:31), as well as the ransom saying of Mark 10:45, indicate that a divine initiative also leads him toward a climactic conflict in Jerusalem.

Luke is equally as forthright in this theme of human and non-human conflict.[19] Jesus' arrival in Jerusalem is greeted by a renewed zeal on the part of the Jerusalem leaders (Lk 19:47–48). Satan enters Judas, who then offers himself as an instrument to bring Jesus to his death (22:1–6). In the hours before the arrest and crucifixion, Luke allows the reader to peer behind the scenes to see the true nature of the conflict. It is the hour "when darkness reigns" (22:53), and Satan moves people toward the final act of desperate conflict. Indeed, in this hour when Satan's power is greatest, the disciples are urged to pray that they might not fall into temptation (22:40, 46; cf. 11:4).

Jesus himself approaches the cross with a heightened sense of conflict. Gone are the days when he sent out the disciples without purse, bag, or sandals. Now they must take purse, bag, cloak, and *sword*—though two are enough (Lk 22:36–38). Jesus, on the Mount of Olives, faces the divine necessity of his coming death (22:42; cf. 22:19–20, 22, 37; 24:26) and interprets it as eschatological trial (*peirasmos*, Lk 22:40, 46; cf. 4:13; 8:13; 11:4; 22:28). The theme of conflict is

---

[19]Cf. Lk 11:14–22, 29–32, 37–52, 53–54; 12:1–3; 13:10–17; 14:1–6; 16:24–25.

underscored by his physical distress (22:44) and the appearance of "an angel from heaven" (22:43), who strengthens him.

DAY OF WRATH, DAY OF TRIUMPH

With different emphases, the Synoptic crucifixion narratives present Jesus in his death as the focal point of forces and events that in the Old Testament are associated with the divine warrior's judgment.

In Mark, the darkness that comes over the land from the sixth to the ninth hour (Mk 15:33) symbolizes the darkness of the Day of the Lord (13:24; cf. Joel 2:2; Am 5:18; 8:9). This is the moment of terrible tribulation preceding the final establishment of God's rule. Jesus, who has referred to the destruction of the temple on the model of its sixth-century destruction by Yahweh through the hands of the Babylonians, is now himself the temple that is destroyed (Mk 14:49; 15:38; cf. Jn 2:19–21) through the instrumentality of human (and cosmic) forces. Just as his disciples will be "delivered up" (*paradidōmi*) during the fearful days of tribulation (Mk 13:9, 11–12), so is Jesus repeatedly "delivered up" in his last hours (14:10, 11, 18, 21, 41, 42, 44; 15:1, 10, 15).[20]

Mark presents Jesus' death as an apocalyptic moment that stands at the turning point of the ages. His death as a "ransom for many" is defined by his suffering the divine judgment for the community of his elect—a judgment defined specifically in terms of what the divine warrior might justly inflict on his own people. Mark points out the irony of Jesus' suffering and death by the repeated references to him as "king" (15:2, 9, 12, 18, 26, 32) and the equally royal appellation "Son of God" (15:39; cf. 1:1; 3:11; 9:7)—both of which suggest one who, like a warrior, might leap on his enemies and thereby save himself (15:31).

---

[20]See R. H. Lightfoot, *The Gospel Message of St. Mark* (Oxford: Clarendon, 1950) 48–49; Allison, *The End of the Ages*, 36.

Jesus' death in Mark also recalls the Servant of Isaiah 52:13–53:12, who by his suffering mysteriously emerges triumphant (Isa 53:12) and executes the Isaianic new Exodus. That typology invites us to think of his death as a sacrifice. But here we must recall that within the Old Testament, sacrifice was part of a broader understanding that life was required for life, and that on occasion, life might be taken by the sword or spear in order to satisfy the holiness of God and effect atonement (cf. Nu 25:6–13).[21] Jesus, by the will and design of God, dies at the climax of eschatological battle, absorbing the piercing darkness of the great tribulation and suffering the wrath of God for the many.[22]

Luke's portrayal of Jesus' death differs from that of Mark and Matthew in that he concentrates on the innocence of Jesus and his obedience to the divine necessity of his death—a plan unwittingly brought to its climax by the enemy. But there are hints that Luke sees this death in terms of the Isaiah's righteous Servant of Yahweh.[23]

The themes of divine warrior and servant that Luke has interwoven into his telling of the Beelzebul controversy are brought to a climax at the cross. The theme of eschatological tribulation is apparent when Luke speaks of the darkness that came over the land from the sixth to the ninth hour (Luke tells us that the sun stopped shining) and of the tearing of the temple veil in two. These signs of the judgment of the Day of the Lord are punctuated by the lament of the people beating their breasts in sorrow as they depart (Lk 23:48).

---

[21]Indeed, it is possible that we should see the ban, or *herem*, of Yahweh's warfare as a sacrifice of the occupants of Canaan in the interest of securing the purity of the land.

[22]See Allison, *The End of the Ages*, for an exploration of themes in the Passion narratives interpreting Jesus' death in terms of the eschatological distress that must precede eschatological redemption. Allison, however, does not relate this theme to the motif of the divine warrior.

[23]Cf. Lk 22:37 with Isa 53:12; Lk 23:35 with Isa 42:1; Lk 23:47 with Isa 53:11.

But Matthew's Gospel accents most clearly the eschatological features of the cross. Matthew has portrayed Jesus as a royal figure being led to the cross, one whose legitimacy as Son will be shown in his obedience to the way of suffering and death. At his arrest, when one of his disciples strikes the high priest's servant with his sword, Jesus introduces but rejects the notion of an eleventh-hour apocalyptic in-breaking of the heavenly forces: "Do you think I cannot call on my Father, and he will at once put at my disposal more than twelve legions of angels?" (Mt 26:55).

While Jesus conforms to the model of the suffering Servant of Yahweh (Mt 20:28), with the fulfillment of that destiny comes a startling manifestation of the Day of Yahweh. Here, more emphatically than in Mark, Matthew tells us that Jesus' death was the hour of eschatological travail in which darkness prevailed over the land (Mt 27:45; cf. Zec 14:6). At the moment Jesus gave up his spirit, the temple veil was torn in two (Mt 27:51), the earth shook (27:51; cf. Zec 14:5), the rocks split (Mt 27:51; cf. Zec 14:4), the tombs opened (Mt 27:52), and many saints who had died were raised to life (27:52; cf. Zec 14:5). The last days are telescoped into this epochal moment. The cosmic significance of the cross is set out in bold relief. And its meaning for salvation history is accented by the tearing of the temple veil, thus symbolizing the end of Israel's sacred cult and the coming destruction of the temple. The Roman centurion and his military companions react with terror, like the ancient enemies of Israel's divine warrior (e.g., Ex 15:15; Isa 13:8), and they confess Jesus as Son of God (Mt 27:54). Jesus—tried, obedient, and the focus of the eschatological travail—emerges as triumphant Son of God.

The triumph of Jesus as the divine warrior also highlights the resurrection accounts. Mark's Gospel ends with a brief account of several women returning to the tomb on the first day of the week and finding it open and empty. Their trembling, bewilderment, and flight from the tomb is consistent with

Mark's theme of failure among the disciples. And the promise of a coming encounter in Galilee leaves the future open—particularly to the victorious return of the Son of Man. But the joyful announcement of the resurrection of Jesus is a triumphant shout shattering the darkness of the crucifixion and resolving the sustained conflict that preceded it. There is no question who has won the eschatological battle—even if the reaction of the women is ironically characterized by the archetypal fear that seizes those who encounter Yahweh as the divine warrior.[24] The victim has emerged the victor.

Matthew tells us that "there was a violent earthquake, for an angel of the Lord came down from heaven, and, going to the tomb, rolled back the stone and sat on it" (Mt 28:2). The two earthquakes—at the crucifixion (27:51) and at the resurrection—seem to indicate that both episodes are part of one event characterized as the Day of the Lord.

But at the resurrection, an angel of the Lord came down from heaven and took part in his vindication. His appearance was striking—like lightning and his clothes as white as wool—suggesting the apocalyptic appearance of a principal angel of God (cf. Da 10:5–6). The guards (*kystōdia* in Mt 27:65–66 and 28:11; *stratiōtēs* in 28:12) shook from fear and became like dead men (28:4), evoking again the classic Old Testament description of Israel's enemies horrified when confronted by the divine warrior. Matthew may also be alluding to this background in recounting the reassuring words of the angel to the women, "Fear not" (*mē phobeisthe*), words frequently

---

[24]The element of fear is thrice repeated in 16:8: *tromos, ekstasis, phobeō*. Mark utilizes *phobos/phobeō* in describing the disciples' reaction to Jesus' stilling the sea (Mk 4:41) and the reaction of the people to the restored man who had been possessed by Legion (5:15). If Mark consciously tells these stories in line with the Exodus motif, the reaction of fear may be an additional feature highlighting a typical human response to the activity of the divine warrior. See Edgar W. Conrad, *Fear Not Warrior: A Study of Pericopes in the Hebrew Scriptures*, BJS, vol. 75 (Chico, Calif.: Scholars, 1985).

addressed to a warrior in the Old Testament (*'al tira'*, "fear not.[O warrior]") or to one beholding a heavenly emissary (cf. Da 10:12, 19).

Matthew's use of the divine-warrior motif culminates in a scene suggesting the enthronement of the victorious Christ. Jesus is exalted to the position of universal sovereign (Mt 28:18b), the heralds are sent forth to proclaim his kingship (28:19–20a), and the security of his enthronement is assured to the end of the age (28:20b).[25] The ancient pattern of the divine warrior's triumph and enthronement has shaped the turning of the ages.

For Luke, the highlight of Christ's victory is his resurrection and exaltation to glory. More than any other Synoptic evangelist, Luke emphasizes the role Satan played in bringing Jesus to the grave. It was a conflict that demanded resolution. And the two steps in Jesus' victory—resurrection and ascension—are bound together in Luke's narrative. In fact, the goal of Jesus' ministry appears to be his victorious ascent into glory (an event referred to earlier in Luke as an *exodus* [Gk *exodos*], cf. 9:31, 51).

In Acts, the account of the ascension is retold as the climactic event of the story of Jesus (Ac 1:1–11). The central kerygma of the message of Peter in Acts 2:14–40 is not the cross but the raising of the one whom death could not hold and his subsequent exaltation to the right hand of the Father (2:24–35). The crucified one has now been made "both Lord and Christ" (2:36). Within Luke's narrative, this emphasis on the victorious exaltation of Jesus stands in contrast with the fall

---

[25]J. Jeremias, *Die Briefe an Timotheus und Titus* (Göttingen: Vandenhoeck & Ruprecht, 1963), 23–24, sees in Mt 28:18–20 the pattern of an oriental, particularly Egyptian, enthronement ceremony in which (1) the new king symbolically receives the divine nature (exaltation), (2) the deified king is presented to the divine council (presentation), and (3) sovereign authority is conferred (enthronement). The scene also recalls Phil 2:6–11; 1 Tim 3:16; and Heb 1:5–14.

of Satan from his heavenly position (Lk 10:18).[26] The emphasis is similar to that of John 12:31–33, which speaks of Jesus being lifted up and the "prince of this world" being driven out. As in the Old Testament, the victorious warrior ascends to his throne and reigns over his enemies.[27]

---

[26]Susan R. Garrett, *The Demise of the Devil: Magic and the Demonic in Luke's Writings* (Minneapolis: Augsburg Fortress, 1989), 51, speaks of Jesus' taking the position at the right hand of God "often thought to have been occupied by Satan." But this seems overly specific, and the reference to Satan thought to be at the right hand of God is puzzling. She also suggests that within Luke's narrative world, Jesus confronts Satan at his exaltation and only then emerges the victor (p. 53). But, we would argue, the tables are turned at the resurrection.

[27]Cf. the apparent exaltation of the angelic warrior Melchizedek, who in the year of the Lord's favor is enthroned in heaven and exacts vengeance from Belial and his spirits (11QMelch). See Garrett, *Demise of the Devil,* 52–53. The text is difficult (cf. P. J. Kobelski, *Milchizedek and Melchiresa',* CBQMS, vol. 10 [Washington, D.C.: The Catholic Biblical Association of America, 1981]).

9

Paul: The Warrior's Defeat of Principalities and Other Powers

THE DIVINE WARRIOR: THE PAULINE PERSPECTIVE

Turning from the Gospels to Paul, we make a transition from the plot of stories to the rhetoric of letters. Nevertheless, Paul has in mind a story of Christ. But like the features of a soaring mountain range obscured by clouds here and there, the story line and features of Paul's narrative of Christ disclose themselves only now and then throughout the situational discourses of his letters.

In telling the story of Christ, Paul utilized the story of God, Israel, and the nations. The progressive pattern of warfare, victory, kingship, temple building, and celebration was transposed. For Paul, God was in Christ reconciling the world; the actions that the Old Testament and Judaism had ascribed to God, Paul could now ascribe to Christ.

The contours of the story are of one sent from heaven to subject the cosmos to its Creator and Lord. Born of a woman (Gal 4:4) and taking human form (Php 2:7), he engaged the enemy, was victorious in an epochal battle (Col 2:15; cf.

1:12–14), and was exalted to God's right hand, where he now reigns as cosmic Lord (1Co 15:24–26; Eph 1:20–22; Php 2:9; Col 3:1; 1Ti 3:16), building his new temple (1Co 3:16–17; 2Co 6:16; Eph 2:19–22), and receiving praise and obeisance (Php 2:10–11). He will come again at the end of the age and conclude his defeat of the enemy, who will have waged a final revolt (2Th 2:8). In the end, death, the final enemy, will stand defeated along with every other hostile power, and Christ will hand over the kingdom to God (1Co 15:24–28). But in the meantime, the people of the Messiah stand between two episodes—climax and resolution—in the eschatological warfare, enjoying the benefits and advantage of Christ's defeat of the enemy at the cross (Ro 8:37). Yet, as they await their Lord to descend from heaven on the final day (1Th 4:16–17), they are still beset by a hostile foe (Eph 6:10–17).

This story of conflict and triumph presumes enemies. And Paul selected and fashioned a rich vocabulary to describe them in their various aspects. These enemies consisted not of Romans or Greeks but of "principalities and powers," sin, flesh, death, law, and a final enemy he called the "man of lawlessness."

THE POWERS

For Paul, the imagery of the Davidic warrior king in Psalm 110:1 was an archetypal image for portraying the exaltation of Christ as victorious Lord. Indeed, from an early period, the church employed this psalm in expressing the significance of Christ and his work, both past and present (Ac 2:33; 5:31; 7:55–56; cf. Mk 12:35–37). Wherever we find reference in the New Testament to the enthroned Lord at the right hand of God, we see the influence of Psalm 110:1. For the psalmist, the enemies who were a footstool for the Lord's feet (an ancient Near Eastern image of submission to a conqueror) were the flesh and blood enemies of Israel that God would subdue and place under submission to a future Davidic king. When

Paul (and the early church) contemplated this in light of the work of Christ, a different picture emerged. The enemies were spiritual, cosmic powers now submitted to the victorious and exalted Christ.

Moreover, in many instances Psalm 8:6 was aligned with Psalm 110:1 (cf. 1Co 15:22–28; Eph 1:19–22; Heb 1:3, 13; 2:8; 1Pe 3:22; cf. Col 3:1–11). The link between the two psalms in their application to Christ was the theme of submission beneath the feet. In Psalm 8 we read of the creational submission of "everything" beneath the feet of humans (*'enôš*; *ben 'adam*) in their royal capacity as vice-regents over creation. In some streams of early Judaism, there was an understanding that Israel–or at least the faithful remnant–was the true heir of the glory of Adam.[1] Paul saw this fulfilled in the redemptive submission of all things (a creation gone astray, including rebellious powers) beneath the feet of the Second Adam, who represented the new people of God and was now reigning in heaven. In most cases Paul refers to the submission of "principalities and powers," but in 1 Corinthians 15 he also speaks of the last enemy, death, which holds the creation in its thrall. We will first look at the principalities and powers, returning later to examine death.

Principalities and powers is shorthand for a variety of terms Paul employed to refer to what most interpreters have concluded to be spiritual cosmic powers: principalities, authorities, powers, dominions, thrones, rulers, and world rulers of this present darkness.[2] In addition, the "elements/

---

[1]The texts are numerous, but include, e.g., 1QS 4:23; CD 3:20; 1QH 17:15. See N. T. Wright, *The Climax of the Covenant* (Minneapolis: Fortress, 1991), 23–25.

[2]I am following RSV language throughout this section: "principalities" (*archai*, Ro 8:38; 1Co 15:24; Eph 1:21; 3:10; 6:12; Col 1:16; 2:10, 15), "authorities" (*exousiai*, 1Co 15:24; Eph 1:21; 2:2; 3:10; 6:12; Col 1:16; 2:10, 15), "powers" (*dynameis*, Ro 8:38; Eph 1:21), "dominions" (*kyriotētes*, Col 1:16; Eph 1:21), "thrones" (*thronoi*, Col 1:16), "rulers" (*archontes*, 1Co 2:6, 8), and "world rulers of this present darkness" (*kosmokratores tou skotous toutou*, Eph 6:12).

elemental spirits of the universe" (*stoicheiai tou kosmou*, Gal 4:3, 9; Col 2:8, 20) and the ambiguous references to angels (*angeloi*, Ro 8:38; cf. 1Co 6:3) may be brought into the picture. Moreover, Paul uses inclusive phrases such as "height" and "depth" (*hypsōma ... bathos*, Ro 8:39), things "visible and invisible" (*ta horata kai ta aorata*, Col 1:16), things "in heaven and on earth and under the earth" (*epouraniōn kai epigeiōn kai katachthoniōn*, Php 2:10), "every name that is named, not only in this age but also in that which is to come" (*pantos onomatos onomazomenou ou monon en tō aiōni toutō alla kai en tō mellonti*, Eph 1:21).

Within the Pauline corpus, these powers are mentioned in a variety of specific contexts, most notably those corresponding to decisive episodes in the story of Christ: they were brought into existence by the preexistent Christ in his creative role (Col 1:16); were led in triumphal procession as defeated enemies at the cross (Col 2:15; cf. 1Co 2:6, 8); were subjected to the triumphant, exalted, and reigning Christ (Eph 1:21; cf. Col 2:10; Php 2:10); and will be destroyed at the eschatological consummation of God's plan (1Co 15:24).

The theme of principalities and powers is particularly significant for understanding the divine-warrior theme in Paul. To grasp their significance, we need to understand the context of first-century Judaism. The Judaism of Paul's day, and Palestinian Judaism in particular, was faced with a long-standing but monumental problem: submission to an occupying power—this time the Romans—who challenged the sanctity of her temple, her territory, and her Torah. More than a social and political problem, this posed a theological problem demanding a theodicy. In fact, so grave was the problem that some Jews regarded this as evidence that Israel—whether in the land or in diaspora—was in reality still in exile (cf. Bar 1:15–3:8; CD 1:5–8)[3] and

---

[3]See J. M. Scott, "Restoration of Israel," in *DPL*, 796–805; N. T. Wright, *The Climax of the Covenant* (Minneapolis: Fortress, 1992), 136–56, 261. For how this problem was viewed by Jews who saw the Maccabean revolt as its resolution, see J. A. Goldstein, "How the Authors of 1 and 2 Maccabees

was awaiting her eschatological deliverance. Among the forms of Judaism contemporary with Paul, the apocalyptic response seems to have been popular. In our discussion of Jesus and the Gospels, we have mentioned the War Scroll (11QM, 4QM 491–496) from Qumran as an outstanding example of how an apocalyptic perspective could refashion the tradition of the divine warrior and holy warfare.

Expanding on the account of eschatological battle described in Daniel 11:40–12:3, the War Scroll depicts on one side the righteous of Israel, called the "Sons of Light," assisted by Michael (1QM 17:7), or the Prince of Light (1QM 13:10–12; cf. CD 5:18),[4] and the angelic forces. On the other side of the conflict are the "Sons of Darkness," who are aligned with Belial and his powers of darkness. Various traditional opponents of Israel (Edom, Moab, Ammon, Philistia, 1QM 1:1–2) are first to be defeated, with the final battle being pitched against the "Kittim of Asshur" (1QM 1:1–14; 11:11; cf. Nu 24:24), probably a reference to the Romans, who encroached on Palestine during the second half of the first century B.C. The War Scroll's appropriation of the language and imagery of divine warfare and of the traditional names of Israel's enemies now fortified by demonic powers, suggests an avenue for understanding Paul's depiction of the powers.

Paul professed that as a Pharisaic Jew he had been zealous for the cause of Israel (Gal 1:13–14; Php 3:5–6), a passion that was transformed by his encounter with the risen Lord (e.g., Ro 9:1–5). With Paul's conversion came a radical reassessment of

---

Treated the 'Messianic' Promises," in *Judaisms and Their Messiahs at the Turn of the Christian Era*, ed. J. Neusner, et al. (Cambridge: Cambridge University Press, 1987), 69–96, esp. 69–74.

[4]The role of the angelic warrior figure in Judaism may be traced back to the "commander of the army of the Lord" who appeared to Joshua (Jos 5:13–15) prior to the conquest of Jericho. On transcendent savior figures in Judaism, see J. J. Collins, "Messianism in the Maccabean Period," in *Judaisms and Their Messiahs*, 97–109, esp. 101–3; C. Rowland, *The Open Heaven* (New York: Crossroad, 1982), 94–103.

the place of Torah, temple, and territory in God's redemptive plan. Moreover, the Gentiles, being formerly reckoned as enemies of God's purpose in history, were now the very people to whom he was called to proclaim the good news of eschatological peace initiated by Jesus Messiah. No longer were the Gentiles typecast as enemies of God, and, like the prophets, Paul could name Israel as God's enemy (Ro 5:10; 8:7; 11:28; Col 1:21; 1Th 2:14–16). Individuals from both Jews and Gentiles were now potentially people of God or enemies of God. Outside of Christ, both were enslaved to the elemental spirits of this age (Gal 4:3, 8–9). Indeed, Paul seems to have reckoned himself as having formerly been an enemy of Christ who had been conquered (2Co 2:14).

In Paul's theology, we find evidence of a hermeneutical shift by which the traditional symbols, or pillars, of Judaism were reinterpreted. Likewise, it appears that the themes of Yahweh the divine warrior and the traditional enemies of Israel were transformed. The Gentiles, who had once been "far away" as aliens and enemies (Eph 2:17; cf. Col 1:21), had now become the focus of God's saving grace. They could no longer be regarded as flesh and blood enemies simply by virtue of their race, nor even because of their occupation of Israel's land of promise. As a matter of fact, the destruction and oppression they had enacted on Israel was part of the Lord's covenant curse against his people (Dt 28:58–68). Paradoxically, the final destruction warned of in the covenant curse had been drawn down on Israel's representative, the Messiah, as he hung on the cross (Gal 3:10–14). His death was Israel's death, and with it was opened up the way for Jews and Gentiles to become one new eschatological person in Christ (cf. Eph 2:14–18).[5] From this perspective, the most formidable enemies were not the Romans, but the spiritual powers that lurked behind the human

---

[5]Here we find agreement with N. T. Wright, *The Climax of the Covenant*, 146, 213.

faces of the authorities and empires of this world. Paradoxically, Paul could speak of Jews who opposed the gospel and rejected the cross of Christ as still under the covenant curse, "heap[ing] up their sins to the limit" and so deserving the coming wrath of God (1Th 2:16; cf. 1:10). This language drew on an image associated with God's judgment on Israel's classic enemies (Ge 15:16; Da 8:23; cf. 2Mc 6:14; Mt 23:32) and may have found its fulfillment in the cataclysm of A.D. 70.[6]

As we mentioned in an earlier chapter, the alignment of spiritual powers and Gentile nations found precedent in the Old Testament:

> When the Most High apportioned the nations,
>   when he divided humankind,
> he fixed the boundaries of the peoples
>   according to the number of the gods;
> the LORD's own portion was his people,
>   Jacob his allotted share. (Dt 32:8–9 NRSV; cf. Sir 17:17; Jub 15:31–32)[7]

The gods and idols of the nations were in reality demons (Dt 32:17; cf. 1Co 10:20), who were to be judged by the Judge of all the earth (Ps 82; Isa 24:21). This understanding of the spiritual powers behind the nations had been further developed in

---

[6]This introduces another interesting aspect of Paul, his apparent understanding of his apostleship in terms of the OT prophetic tradition. See C. A. Evans, "Prophet, Paul as," in *DPL*, 762–65; K. O. Sandnes, *Paul–One of the Prophets? A Contribution to the Apostle's Self-Understanding*, WUNT, vol. 2 (Tübingen: Mohr, 1991), 43. Germane to our topic is the prophetic application of Israel's tradition to new situations, emphasizing God's point of view, not ethnocentric "peace and safety." Thus, the divine warrior who defeated Israel's enemies will turn against Israel (cf. Isa 28:21–22 with 2Sa 5:17–25). Paul can take an imprecation formerly declaimed against Israel's enemies (Ps 69:22–23) and turn it back on Israel (Rom 11:9–10). See C. A. Evans, "Paul and the Hermeneutics of 'True Prophecy': A Study of Romans 9–11," *Bib* 65 (1984): 560–70.

[7]Paul develops the notion of Israel as the "inheritance" of Yahweh when he speaks of the church as God's "inheritance" in Eph 1:18. This allusion, set within the context of Christ's exaltation over the powers, further supports our interpretation that Paul associated the powers with the nations.

Daniel's vision of the monstrous beasts representing empires (Da 7:2–8) and the "Prince" of Persia and Greece, who was resisted by "the one like a man" and Michael, the Prince of Israel (10:13, 20–21). And there is evidence that Paul shared this perspective with other Jews of his era.[8]

Just as the holy angels serve the most high God, so for Paul and his Jewish antecedents, the evil spiritual powers serve their lord, variously known as Mastema, Beliar/Belial, Azazel, Satan, the Devil, or the angel of darkness. Paul can speak of this ruler of the kingdom of darkness as "Satan" (*satanas*: Ro 16:20; 1Co 5:5; 7:5; 2Co 2:11; 11:14; 12:7; 1Th 2:18; 2Th 2:9; cf. 1Ti 1:20; 5:15), "Belial" or "Beliar" (2Co 6:15), or the "god of this age" (2Co 4:4; cf. Ac 26:18). In Ephesians and the Pastorals, he is also called "the devil" (*diabolos*, "slanderer" or "adversary": Eph 4:27; 6:11; 1Ti 3:6, 7, 11; 2Ti 2:26; 3:3; Tit 2:3), perhaps reflecting a later linguistic habit of Paul. Certainly, the New Testament gives clear evidence that the terms were interchangeable (note the variety in Revelation), and Ephesians aligns the principalities and powers with "the devil" (Eph 6:11), who should probably be identified as the "ruler of the kingdom of the air, the spirit who is now at work in those who are disobedient" (Eph 2:2; cf. 2Co 4:4). The Devil, or Satan, is the archenemy of Christ and his church and makes personal attacks on Paul and his congregations.

In Romans 16:20, Paul expresses his confidence that "the God of peace will soon crush Satan under your feet." The influence of Genesis 3:15 is clearly present here. But it is "the God of peace," not Christ, who will defeat the enemy. Genesis 3:15 speaks of the seed of the woman crushing the head of the

---

[8]Cf. Jub 15:30–32; 1En 89:59–61; 90:20–25, where the seventy shepherds seem to represent the angels of the nations (cf. Isa 24:21). G. W. E. Nickelsburg has argued that the author of the Parables of Enoch has as a "principle concern ... the persecution of the righteous by kings and rulers who are the embodiment of demonic forces." See his "Salvation Without and With a Messiah: Developing Beliefs in Writings Ascribed to Enoch," in *Judaisms and Their Messiahs*, 62; cf., 57.

serpent. In speaking of God as the subject and Satan "under your feet," Paul seems to be mixing allusions to Genesis 3:15 with Psalm 110:1 and/or Psalm 8:6. The latter is the more likely text, since it speaks of God placing the created order under the superintendence of humankind as vice-regent. On this reading, Paul would be saying that in defeating Satan, who leads and epitomizes creation in rebellion, God will be restoring to the children of the Last Adam their role of dominion and eschatological *shalom*.

The powers populate the conflicted backdrop of the Pauline drama of redemption, appearing among the potential barriers to the love of Christ (Ro 8:38). In Ephesians, they are even more boldly presented as the enemies of Christ who oppose the church in the present age (Eph 6:12). From their vantage point "in the heavenly realms," however, they observe God's wisdom unfolding in his plan for the ages (3:10). Interpreters have questioned whether the principalities and powers are in fact personal, spiritual beings who are irredeemably evil.[9] Could their evil perhaps arise out of the honor, sovereignty, and power that humans grant them over their lives? Might they represent the oppressive social structures and ideologies that hold peoples and nations in their thrall? It is difficult, however, to reconcile either of these interpretations with the immediate context of a text like 1 Corinthians 15:24–26, where the powers are listed among the eschatological "enemies" (*echthroi,* 1Co 15:25–26; cf. Eph 6:12), including death, that in the end will be destroyed (*katargeō*). Just as death will not be reconciled or redeemed for the good of the kingdom, so the powers seem to be relegated to the eschatological "ban" of Yahweh's war.

---

[9]See, e.g., W. Wink, *Naming the Powers* (Philadelphia: Fortress, 1984); and more recently N. T. Wright, *The Epistles of Paul to the Colossians and to Philemon,* TNTC, vol. 12 (Grand Rapids: Eerdmans, 1987), 100–118.

In four instances Paul uses the term *stoicheia* (three times "of the universe," *tou kosmou*; see Gal 4:3, 9; Col 2:8, 20; cf. Heb 5:12; 2Pe 3:10, 12) in a way that has led some interpreters to conclude that it is part of the field of enemies. Usually translated as either "elements of this world" or "elemental spirits of this world," the difference discloses the interpretive issue of whether Paul had in mind something animate or inanimate. We know that the term *stoicheion* had been used in many contexts, and the related term *stoichos* was used in military contexts in the sense of a "row," "rank," or "line." *Stoicheion* came to refer to things in a series, the basic rudiments of a subject, and to the basic elements of the physical world–earth, air, water, fire. It was used in reference to star deities, demons, and angels.[10] Paul's usage must ultimately determine his meaning, and, of course, he need not have used the term in the same way in both Galatians and Colossians. But there are basic similarities in all four usages, and there are indications that he was referring to animate spiritual beings.

In Colossians 2:8–10, Paul refers to a false teaching that is "according to the *stoicheia tou kosmou*" rather than "according to Christ," who is the head of every principality and power. Later he speaks of the Colossians as having died with Christ "from the *stoicheia tou kosmou*" (2:20), with all of their encumbering and ineffective rules and regulations. In Galatians, the *stoicheia tou kosmou* first refers to Jewish religion characterized by the law (Gal 4:3) and then (*stoicheia* as "weak and miserable") to pagan religion (4:9) presided over by "those who by nature are not gods" (4:8). Both systems were in their own way characterized by rules and regulations and the servility of humans (cf. 4:3, 10). Perhaps the term was Paul's special way of referring to local or national deities who rule over territories and races. Akin to the principalities and powers, *stoicheia tou kosmou* may have been Paul's way of getting at the subject from another

---

[10]See G. Delling, "στοιχεῖον," *TDNT* 7.670–83.

angle, that of basic allegiances at the ethnic and tribal level.[11] But certainty regarding its meaning seems ever to elude us.

If the powers played a role such as we have been describing in Paul's narrative of Christ and the politics of the cosmos, they were also known in individual experience as the hostile cosmic powers of the universe who gripped with fear the hearts of many in Paul's world. Whether through association with magic, the mysteries, or astrology, popular religion of the first-century Mediterranean world conceived of a cosmos haunted by spirits in the heavens, on the earth, and beneath the earth.[12]

Paul addressed this situation by announcing that the powers of darkness had been defeated by Christ on the cross. Though their power was still real and potent even after the cross, they were not to be feared by those "in Christ" (Ro 8:37–39). In Christ, believers had died to the elemental powers of the world (Col 2:20) or, in an image reminiscent of the Exodus, had been redeemed from slavery to those elemental spirits, whether the context be Judaism or any other tribal religion (Gal 4:3–9). Thus, when Paul spoke of the hostility of the powers in this age and their defeat by Christ, he spoke a language that was not only fundamentally Jewish in its echo of Old Testament archetypes and the pattern of redemption, but one that met fear with liberation in the hearts of his Gentile audience.

THE DEFEAT OF THE POWERS AT THE CROSS

How did Paul conceive of these powers being defeated? Colossians 2:14–15 is the closest we come to an answer. Paul locates the triumph of Christ at the cross; of that we can be sure. But the interpretation of this passage involves a number of

---

[11]See G. B. Caird, *Paul's Letters from Prison* (Oxford: Oxford University Press, 1976), 190, and Wright, *Colossians and Philemon,* 101–2.

[12]See C. Arnold, *Powers of Darkness: Principalities and Powers in Paul's Letters* (Downers Grove, Ill.: InterVarsity Press, 1992).

complex issues, some of which cannot be explored here.[13] But a certain amount of complexity must be endured to explain our conclusion.

In pursuit of our theme, we focus on Colossians 2:15, where the powers are named and the triumph of Christ is proclaimed. With some commentators, we detect a shift from God to Christ as subject in 2:14–15. A fundamental issue is whether the verb Paul employs (*apekdyomai*) tells us that Jesus stripped himself or stripped the powers of something. To put it in grammatical terms, is *apekdysamenos,* which is middle in form, a true middle voice (the subject acting on itself), or is it only middle in form but active in meaning (the subject acting on someone or something else)? Which did Paul have in mind?

The term is not used in the New Testament outside of Colossians, but the context·comes to our aid. Paul has already used the related noun *apekdysis* a few verses earlier in Colossians 2:11, where he speaks of the believer's circumcision in Christ's "putting off of the sinful nature." This was the "circumcision done by Christ." This circumcision (as an objective genitive) most likely refers to Christ's death on the cross, in which believers participate by baptism (2:12). It is the "circumcision" Christ himself underwent when he reconciled believers "by Christ's physical body through death" (1:22). So, in using the noun *apekdysis,* Paul engages a metaphor alluding to Christ's death on the cross and leaves unanswered the question "Who did it?" Later, in 3:9, Paul uses the verb again, in the same participial form as in 2:15 (this time plural, *apekdysamenoi*), to refer to something that takes place in the

---

[13]See E. Lohse, *Colossians and Philemon,* Hermeneia (Philadelphia: Fortress, 1971); R. P. Martin, *Colossians and Philemon,* NCB, 3d ed. (Grand Rapids: Eerdmans, 1981); idem, *Colossians: The Church's Lord and the Christian's Liberty* (London: Paternoster, 1972); C. F. D. Moule, *The Epistles of Paul to the Colossians and to Philemon,* CGTC (Cambridge, Eng.: University Press, 1957); P. T. O'Brien, *Colossians, Philemon,* WBC, vol. 44 (Waco: Word, 1982); E. Schweizer, *The Letter to the Colossians* (Minneapolis: Augsburg, 1982); Wright, *Colossians and Philemon.*

experience of believers: those in Christ are to undergo an ethical renewal (3:8), logically implied in their having "put off" their old humanity (*ton palaion anthrōpon*, 3:9) and "put on" (*endysamenoi*) their new humanity in Christ (3:10). That is to say, in their baptism/circumcision with Christ (2:11–13), they died to, or shed their identification with, the old Adamic humanity and took on the new humanity that is defined by the New Adam, Christ.

It is reasonable to assume that Paul in Colossians 2:15 uses *apekdyomai* as a true middle, thus establishing a parallel between what Christ had done on the cross and what was also to be true of Christian experience. Christ did not strip the powers, divesting them of their weaponry or clothing; in dying on the cross, he stripped off the principalities and powers from himself. In this way the cross was an instrument not of shame but of triumph.[14]

But how could Paul speak of Christ stripping off the powers—as if they were a garment? This interpretation seems to leave a premise unstated; and if it is unstated, how can we fill it in with confidence? Again, the context comes to our aid. The Colossians faced an apparently persuasive religious alternative that Paul refers to as being according to "the basic principles of this world [*stoicheia tou kosmou*]" and not according to Christ (2:8), who is the head of all principalities and powers (2:10). But, Paul reminds them, they have been "circumcised" not by human hands, but in the "putting off" (*apekdysis*) of the "sinful nature" (lit., "body of flesh," *sōmatos tēs sarkos*) in the circumcision of Christ (2:11). Paul makes it clear that this "circumcision done by Christ" is their participation in the death/burial and resurrection of Christ ritually portrayed in their baptism (2:12).

[14]See J. B. Lightfoot, *St. Paul's Epistles to the Colossians and to Philemon* (London: Macmillan, 1879); J. A. T. Robinson, *The Body: A Study in Pauline Theology*, SBT, vol. 5 (London: SCM, 1952), 41; C. A. A. Scott, *Christianity According to St. Paul* (Cambridge, Eng.: University Press, 1961), 34–35.

In this participation with Christ, they have passed from a state of death in their trespasses to life in divine forgiveness (2:13). As Paul will remind them several verses later, they have died with Christ out from under the dominion and active influence of "the basic spirits of this world" (2:20), with their impotent and codified religious demands (2:16–23).

Participation in the death and resurrection of Christ has liberated the Colossians from the elemental spirits of the world, otherwise known as the principalities and powers. This is true of believers because Christ himself triumphed over the powers on the cross. His death was a bodily death–and a bloody one too, like the rite of circumcision. Christ, having taken on human flesh in his solidarity with humankind, but more particularly with Israel, took on the weakness of the flesh (cf. Ro 8:3). He was thereby made subject to the demands, accusations, and schemes of the powers of evil. In an allusion that may have had special significance for the believers at Colossae, Paul states that Christ took away the handwritten documentation of their charge against men and women by nailing it, so to speak, to the cross (Col 2:14).[15] What was nailed to the cross was Christ's body of flesh. That was the very point at which he shared with and stood in for Israel in particular, and humans more generally, as the powers unleashed their assault. But because he was obedient and without sin, his death was in fact a triumph (2:15). The picture is analogous to the divine warrior's leading foreign kings and their armies against Jerusalem and the people of God, here represented by the Messiah. But Jesus, like the temple destroyed and rebuilt (Jn 2:18–22; cf. Mk 14:57–58; 15:29–30; Mt 26:61; 27:40), absorbed the onslaught of the powers and thereby triumphed over them.

---

[15]For arguments and evidence for this interpretation, see the commentaries, especially R. P. Martin, *Colossians: The Church's Lord and the Christian's Liberty* (Grand Rapids: Zondervan, 1972).

This is a bold metaphor indeed, pointing out the paradox and irony of the cross in a vivid image. Paul is not flirting with Gnostic notions of the fleshly body as evil per se (although Gnostics would later appropriate the image, see *Gospel of Truth* 20.20–23). He develops the theme that is elsewhere expressed as Christ's solidarity with Adam's race, the old humanity (Ro 5:12–21). And he balances it with another aspect of Christ's work on the cross, the forgiveness of sins (Col 2:13–14). This Adam-Christ analogy is clearly on Paul's mind when he applies this theological lesson to the Colossians' conduct, for he reminds them that they too have "put off" the "old self" (*palaion anthrōpon*, 3:9). In so speaking, he refers to their "dead" but still assertive lineage of the old humanity and its entanglements with the old aeon in its social and spiritual dimensions (cf. Ro 6:6; Gal 5:24).[16]

The triumph Paul is pointing to is this: Christ in his death as the obedient second Adam turned the tables on the powers of evil and defeated their purposes, publicly displaying (*edeigmatisen en parrēssia*, Col 2:15) their true and shameful nature.[17] Just as a criminal justice system is exposed in its shortcomings when it executes an innocent person, so much more were the cosmic powers exposed and defeated when they crucified the sinless Lord of glory. The victory celebrated is, at its heart, not the victory of a more powerful being over less powerful beings (as if it were a cosmic struggle of strength against strength in which salvation was achieved by a tour de force); it is the victory of holy, righteous, and creative love over the destructive forces of evil.

---

[16]On this aspect of "flesh," see J. M. G. Barclay, *Obeying the Truth: Paul's Ethics in Galatians* (Minneapolis: Fortress, 1991), 202–15.

[17]For ancient thinking about publicly shaming one's enemy, see S. K. Stowers, "Friends and Enemies in the Politics of Heaven: Reading Theology in Philippians," in *Pauline Theology* Vol. 1: *Thessalonians, Philippians, Galatians, Philemon*, ed. J. M. Bassler (Minneapolis: Fortress, 1991), 105–21, esp. 113–14.

But as Paul's statements in other contexts will make it plain, he does not mean that the cross was the last chapter in the warfare against the powers of this age. It was an epochal victory, the climax of a cosmic battle. But the enemy is still hostile and active, posing a threat to the church (Eph 6:10–18). On the final day, this battle will reach its resolution, after Christ "has destroyed all dominion, authority and power," along with "the last enemy," death (1Co 15:24, 26).

Thriambeuō, the Greek verb translated "triumphing" in Colossians 2:15, is the Greek term for the Roman triumphal march in which a victorious general or ruler in ceremonial dress and riding a splendid chariot drawn by four horses would drive his captives—most importantly, those who had held authority and power—and spoils of war before him, through the Porta Triumphalis and into Rome. There the prisoners, or representatives of their number, were customarily executed.[18] In this processional, the glory and power of Rome were celebrated and reaffirmed with the triumphant general, who was made up as the great god Jupiter and played the part of the supreme god who had blessed him with fortune in war; to Jupiter thanks would be rendered on reaching the procession's goal, the temple of Jupitor Capitolinus.[19]

The Roman triumph was an image that Paul applied to Christ on more than one occasion, as is evident from his allusion to it in 2 Corinthians 2:14. There he pictures himself as led in the triumphal procession of Christ. But the image is not of Paul as one of the high-ranking officers in Christ's army. For, as S. J. Hafemann has convincingly argued, Paul's speaking of himself being led in triumph (*thriambeuonti hēmas*) can mean

---

[18]S. J. Hafemann, *Suffering and Ministry in the Spirit: Paul's Defense of His Ministry in 2 Corinthians 2:14–3:3* (Grand Rapids: Eerdmans, 1990), 19–34; H. S. Versnel, *Triumphus* (Leiden: Brill, 1970); L. Williamson, "Led in Triumph: Paul's Use of *Thriambeuo*," *Int* 22 (1968): 317–32. Cf. R. B. Egan, "Lexical Evidence on Two Pauline Passages," *NovT* 19 (1977): 34–62.

[19]Cf. Josephus, *J. W.* 7 §§153–55.

nothing other than that he reckoned himself as one of Christ's former enemies who had been conquered and was now marched as a captive, being constantly led to his death![20]

In Colossians 2:15, Paul boldly affirms that Christ, contrary to his appearance as humiliated and defeated on the cross, actually led his enemies in triumph from the cross. In J. B. Lightfoot's memorable phrase, "The paradox of the crucifixion is thus placed in its strongest light—triumph in helplessness and glory in shame. The convict's gibbet is the victor's car."[21] The foreground imagery is Greco-Roman, but its substructure centers on Christ, who fulfills the Jewish archetype of Israel's divine warrior and vanquishes his foes.

The story behind this scenario at the cross is alluded to in 1 Corinthians 2:6–8. Speaking of the wisdom of God (epitomized by the cross of Christ) compared to the "wisdom of this age," Paul writes that "the rulers of this age" did not comprehend the secret, hidden wisdom of God, "for if they had, they would not have crucified the Lord of glory." In speaking of "rulers," Paul uses the Greek word *archontes*, a term commonly used of human rulers (Ro 13:3) and not mentioned in Paul's other listings of "principalities and powers." Although the interpretation that Paul here refers to spiritual powers has been challenged,[22] there is good extra-Pauline evidence, based on the use of *archontes* to speak of spiritual powers in the Greek text of Daniel 10, that Paul was referring to spiritual, cosmic powers in 1 Corinthians 2:6, 8. [23]

---

[20]S. J. Hafemann, *Suffering and Ministry in the Spirit*, 16–34.

[21]Lightfoot, *St. Paul's Epistles to the Colossians and Philemon.*

[22]G. D. Fee argues for a reference to human rulers only. See Fee, *The First Epistle to the Corinthians*, NICNT (Grand Rapids: Eerdmans, 1987), 103–5; idem, *New Testament Exegesis: A Handbook for Students and Pastors* (Philadelphia: Westminster, 1983), 87–92.

[23]See Da 10:13, where the Masoretic text uses the Hebrew *sar* ("chief," "prince," "captain" or "rule?") of Michael, and the LXX and Theodotion have *heis tōn archontōn tōn prōtōn* ("one of the prominent rulers"). Cf. also Theodotion with *archōn* (singular) used of Michael in Da 10:21 and 12:1,

Thus, in 1 Corinthians 2, when Paul speaks of the *archontes tou aionos toutou* ("rulers of this age"), he may have had in mind or been influenced by the Danielic cosmology of spiritual powers lying behind the nations. He could easily have used *archontes* as a general term for the hostile spiritual powers who, as the chief proponents of "the wisdom of this age," were oblivious to the wisdom of God's plan for the ages (cf. Eph 3:10) and so crucified the Lord of glory. As we have seen, the motif of satanic opposition to Jesus is firmly woven into the Gospel tradition, and we can justly surmise that it represented a widespread early Christian understanding of the spiritual conflict that stood behind the human opposition that led Jesus to the cross. This background found in 1 Corinthians sheds interpretive light on how Paul could have envisioned Christ's triumph (Col 2:15) as a victory over unsuspecting powers.

THE DEFEAT OF THE POWERS
ON THE DAY OF THE LORD

Paul speaks of the ultimate defeat of the powers in 1 Corinthians 15:24. The context of their defeat is the Parousia of Christ and the final resurrection of those in Christ (1Co 15:23). Paul is expressing a linear and logical order of events. When Christ comes, then will come the end or goal (*telos*), when Christ delivers the kingdom to God the Father. But this will only take place *after* he has destroyed every principality, authority, and power—the last enemy to be destroyed being death (15:24, 26). The reason Christ does not deliver the kingdom over to the Father before then is that Christ must reign until "he has put all enemies under his feet." Here Paul appeals to Psalm 110:1, working its language into his argument as if it

---

where the LXX has *angelos*. In LXX Da 10:20–21 the spiritual ruler (Heb. *šar*) of Persia and of Greece is a *stratēgos* ("captain"), while Theodotion consistently uses *archōn*. See D. G. Reid, "Principalities and Powers," in *DPL*, 746–52.

needed no explanation. But who is the "he" that will set all enemies under Christ's feet? The psalm indicates it is God, but Paul's grammar would suggest that it is Christ himself. The latter is probably correct.[24] Christ must finish his work of subjecting the powers to his authority and destroying them, the final power being death, which cannot be destroyed until the very end.

Paul then echoes the language of Psalm 8:6, "for 'he has put everything under his feet'" (1Co 15:27), thus indicating Christ's fulfillment of his role as last Adam. But again we are faced with the problem of identifying the subject of the sentence, "he." In this case, it appears to be God, who ultimately stands behind Christ's triumph over the powers and who has subjected all things to "him," that is, Christ, the last Adam, who fulfills the role of humanity in Psalm 8. Paul therefore joins the fulfillment of the work of Christ as divine warrior with the theme of the new creation. Here is a Christological intensification of the Old Testament theme of creation rejuvenated at the triumph of God.

THE DEFEAT OF DEATH

When Paul speaks of death as "the last enemy" (1Co 15:26), he speaks a truth to which most people would nod their assent. But Paul had in mind more than the fear of death common to humankind. He was making a theological point. Death is not natural to the cosmos as it was created by God. It is an intruder, an enemy. More than a human enemy, it is a cosmic enemy encompassing humankind and the whole creation.[25] Death is also more than a *physical* reality; it is a *moral* and *spiritual* reality. Even though believers may experience in Christ a

---

[24]For a discussion of the subject in this passage, see G. D. Fee, *The First Epistle to the Corinthians*, 755–57.

[25]C. Beker, *Paul the Apostle: The Triumph of God in Life and Thought* (Philadelphia: Fortress, 1980), 221–22.

release from death in a spiritual sense, they continue to experience suffering, disease, affliction, and eventually, physical death—because of sin and their solidarity with creation, which is awaiting its final release from bondage to decay (Ro 8:18–25). Thus, death is also an *eschatological* reality.

Paul argues in Romans 5 that death entered the world through sin and cast its dark shadow over all humanity since Adam. Thus, sin was prior to death, and Paul can even speak of death as the wages that the cruel master, sin, pays its servants (Ro 6:23). Death established its sovereignty, reigning from Adam to Jesus Christ (5:14, 21). It has so permeated the human situation that Paul can write, "to set the mind on the flesh is death" (8:6). That is to say, those whose minds are directed toward what is earthly, physical, and passing away are in a state of death. Death characterizes "this age" as opposed to the "age to come," which for Paul is characterized by life. From this perspective, we can see why Paul could speak of death as a personified enemy with a sovereignty and power even greater than that of the principalities and powers.

The general theme of death as a personified, even mythological, enemy was not coined by Paul. In the ancient Near East, death was viewed by some as an actively hostile power who lived in the non-world of the grave, the ocean, or the desert, from which it made its intrusions into life in the form of sickness, bad luck, poverty, and imprisonment. Such thinking is expressed in the Old Testament in the motif of Sheol. It is also present in texts from early Judaism (e.g., 4Ezr 8:53).[26] Paul himself draws on an Old Testament expression of this idea found in Hosea 13:14, where Yahweh calls on Death and Sheol to carry out his grim judgment against Ephraim:

---

[26]See M. C. de Boer, *The Defeat of Death*, JSNTSup, vol. 22 (Sheffield: JSOT, 1988) for details.

I will ransom them from the power of the grave
I will redeem them from death.
Where, O death, where are your plagues?
Where, O grave, is your destruction?

In 1 Corinthians 15:54–55, Paul adopts the last two lines of Hosea 13:14. But he introduces it with an adaptation from Isaiah 25:8, "Death has been swallowed up in victory," which comes from the hymn of thanksgiving following Isaiah's vivid picture of the divine warrior's epiphany on the Day of the Lord (Isa 24). It is notable that in Isaiah these words about the defeat of death on Mount Zion follow (with an interlude of thanksgiving) after Yahweh's defeat and punishment of "the powers in the heavens above and the kings on the earth below" (Isa 24:21). Paul's use of Isaiah at this point supports his ordering of eschatological events and confirms our thesis that Paul is reinterpreting divine-warrior tradition and the place of the nations and their gods in his development of the principalities and powers (note the correspondence between the powers of the heavens and of earth).

Paul goes on to quote and alter the lines from Hosea by substituting the words "victory" for "plagues," "death" for "grave," and "sting" for "destruction." Thus transformed, these lines are brought into agreement with Isaiah. What once, in the context of Hosea, spelled out the divine summons of the scourge of death (the Hebrew *mwt*, "death," perhaps evoking the Canaanite god Mot, "Death") against Ephraim,[27] now has become a victory taunt over the enemy:

"Death has been swallowed up in victory."
Where, O death, is your victory?
Where, O death, is your sting? (1Co 15:54–55)

Paul caps this declaration with a thanksgiving that underscores the fact that Christ's triumph over death is a victory originating

---

[27]Following the translation of NRSV, not NIV. See D. A. Hubbard, *Hosea*, TOTC (Downers Grove, Ill.: InterVarsity Press, 1989), 222–23.

in God (cf. 2Co 5:19): "Thanks be to God! He gives us the victory through our Lord Jesus Christ" (1Co 15:57). The eschatological work of Yahweh has been and will be carried out by Jesus Messiah.

In only one other place in Paul's letters is Christ's conquest of death stated so boldly. Second Timothy 1:10, speaking of the saving power and grace of God, states: "It has now been revealed through the appearing of our Savior, Jesus Christ, who has destroyed death and has brought life and immortality to light through the gospel." The "appearing" (*epiphaneia*) of Christ is the same word used of Christ's Parousia in 2 Thessalonians 2:18. Here it is used of Jesus' incarnation and highlights that event as a divine visitation (cf. 2Mc 2:24; 14:15; 15:27) by the "Savior." The Greco-Roman world of Paul's day knew many saviors, including Isis and Sarapis, gods renowned for their ability to save humans from mortality. In contrast, Christ has appeared as Savior and destroyed (*katargeō*) death. Here is a piece of realized eschatology, stating the already present reality of Christ's triumph over the last enemy—without distinguishing the temporal order of events as in 1 Corinthians 15.

THE APOCALYPTIC POWER ALLIANCE: DEATH, SIN, FLESH, AND LAW

Returning to the conclusion of Paul's celebration of the conquest of death in 1 Corinthians 15:54–57, he develops Hosea's theme of the "sting" of death. For Paul, this provides an opportunity to move from the future to the present work of Christ: "The sting of death is sin, and the power of sin is the law" (1Co 15:56). The cosmic enemy Death, like a scorpion (cf. Rev 9:20), finds its fatal entry into human life through its sting, sin. And the power by which this poisonous sting takes effect is the law! That is, it is the law, good in itself (Ro 7:12), that makes sin evident and provokes further sin (Ro 5:13, 20; 7:7–25).

◆ 157 ◆

In other words, Paul develops a roster of enemies that we face, to which he elsewhere adds one more, "flesh" (Ro 6:12).[28] Sin, flesh, law, and death, what J. C. Beker has called Paul's "apocalyptic power alliance,"[29] provide another field of enemies against which Christ's triumph may be viewed. If in speaking of the principalities and powers, Paul begins with the political alliances of the cosmos and unfolds their impact on humankind, the personified powers of sin, flesh, law, and death begin from an anthropocentric perspective and reach out to the cosmic dimensions of that predicament–death.

In Romans 5–7, Paul casts the alliance of sin, flesh, law, and death in a narrative of conflict and subsequent defeat. Sin, for Paul, is a supple term; it can refer to acts of disobedience or to a power that holds men and women in its thrall. Sin as a power "entered the world," and along with it came "death" (5:12). It was in the world before the law (5:13), and so "death reigned from the time of Adam to the time of Moses" (5:14) and even until Christ (5:17). The reigns of sin and death are intertwined, so that Paul can say that "sin reigned in death" (5:21) and that sin was the master and humankind was the slave (cf. 5:6, 14). Moreover, it is in the flesh that sin finds its foothold (6:12; cf. 8:6–7) and grasps ready weapons (*hopla*) of wickedness rather than weapons of righteousness (6:13). Sin preys on people, awaiting the opportunity to make the law a bridgehead (*aphormē* in 7:8 could carry this military sense) into humans and so wage war (*antistrateuō*, 7:23) and take individuals prisoner (*aichmalōtizō*, 7:23). For those who in this wretched condition cry out in lament for a deliverer, God an-

---

[28]The NIV translates the Greek word *sarx* in various creative ways, such as "flesh," "sinful nature," "body," "sinful man," etc. We will use the word "flesh" for our designation of this word.

[29]J. C. Beker, *Paul the Apostle,* 189–192. Cf. E. P. Sanders's understanding that Paul's analysis of the human predicament is humanity's existence under the lordship of sin and its need to be transferred to the lordship of Christ. See Sanders, *Paul and Palestinian Judaism* (Philadelphia: Fortress, 1977), 499–500.

swers–"through Jesus Christ our Lord" (7:24–25; cf. 1Co 15:57)!

God initiated the deliverance by sending his own Son in the likeness of sinful flesh (*sarx*, Ro 8:3), and in so doing, the Son entered into sin's sphere of dominion. But when sin pressed its claim on Christ, he, being guiltless, condemned sin in the flesh (8:3). So Christ, coming as the last Adam, conquered sin on its own ground and reversed the condemnation sin had brought on Adam (5:18). The "condemning" of sin carries forensic overtones, but we should not limit the image to the law court.[30] It refers also to the execution of that judgment in the decisive defeat of the power of sin in the death of Christ.

Paul may be playing again here the theme we have noted in 1 Corinthians 2:6–8 and Colossians 2:14–15. The sinless Son entered hostile, enemy-held territory. The enemy, mistaking his likeness of flesh for sinful flesh, sought to destroy this Adam with death. But the death of the Son on the cross was sin's own defeat and destruction.[31] This drama of rescue is similar to that summed up in Galatians 1:4 ("who gave himself for our sins to rescue us from the present evil age") and Colossians 1:13–14 ("he has rescued us from the dominion of darkness and brought us into the kingdom of the Son he loves, in whom we have redemption, the forgiveness of sins").

Thus, the anthropocentric alliance of powers–sin, flesh, law, and death–is defeated in a story in which Christ, as the last Adam, overthrows the enemy in a triumph of righteousness. The theme of the divine warrior has shaded off into a conflict in which the protagonist comes not as a transcendent

---

[30]De Boer, in *Defeat of Death*, differentiates between forensic and cosmological apocalyptic eschatology in Judaism. He speaks of Paul's entering into conversation with the forensic type in Romans and adopting its categories to some extent. Nevertheless, Paul's Christologically determined apocalyptic eschatology is essentially cosmological in perspective, and this is his overriding framework.

[31]See R. Leivestad, *Christ the Conqueror* (London: SPCK, 1954), 119.

figure riding the clouds, but as the one truly righteous man sent by God.

Perhaps we push Paul's words too far in discussing this Adam story under our topic of the divine warrior.[32] But, as we have seen, in describing the exalted Christ, Paul himself freely associates Psalm 8:6 and its Adamic motif with Psalm 110:1 and its divine-warrior motif (1Co 15:25-27). So for Paul, the story of the two Adams, first and last, is not divorced from a more dynamic portrayal of Christ's triumph.

There are Jewish precedents (though without the universal implications of "Adam") for this thinking. We find it in the "son of man" in Daniel, Enoch (1En 46:1-5; who is also the "righteous one," 38:2; cf. 39:6; 53:6), and various notions of an "image," or human appearance, of God or one of his envoys in heaven.[33] For Paul, the Jewish archetype of a human "image" in heaven may have coalesced with his understanding of Christ when he encountered the exalted and glorious Christ on the Damascus Road.[34] The exalted conqueror of the cross bore a human face; the seed of the woman had conquered the serpent (Ge 3:15; Ro 16:20).

We have seen that in Romans and 1 Corinthians Paul speaks of the law as part of this alliance of anthropocentric powers. Though the law in and of itself is holy, just, and good (Ro 7:12), when viewed from the perspective of the human predicament, it serves and empowers sin (7:8, 11; 1Co 15:56).

---

[32]But note the flexibility of the motif within Judaism in its application to the "Word" (Wisdom) in Wisdom of Solomon 18:14-16. There God's "all-powerful word leaped from heaven, from the royal throne," as "a stern warrior carrying the sharp sword of [God's] authentic command" (NRSV) and put to death Egypt's firstborn.

[33]See S. Kim, *The Origin of Paul's Gospel* (Grand Rapids: Eerdmans, 1982), 137-268; A. Segal, *Paul the Convert* (New Haven: Yale University Press, 1990), 34-71.

[34]Cf. Christ as the "image of God" in 2Co 4:4 (cf. Col 1:15 and perhaps the "very nature [of] God" in Php 2:6) with the Acts accounts of Paul's vision of Jesus of Nazareth in his blinding glory (Ac 9:3-6; 22:6-9; 26:13-15). See Kim, *Origins*, 193-94.

Paul also says that the law increases the consciousness of sin (Ro 3:20) and brings God's wrath on humankind (4:15). Sin perverts the law, and the law is powerless to overcome the flesh (8:3). Christ did what the law was unable to do and overcame sin.

Within this narrative view of the powers, the law is a circumstantial accomplice in a cosmic revolt. Within the polemical context of Galatians, in which the ritual and ethical norms of the law threatens to undermine the believers' identity and pattern of behavior in Christ,[35] Paul portrays the law in an apocalyptic scenario in which it serves as an inimical force.[36] Within the history of salvation, it was "added because of transgressions" (Gal 3:19), acted as a jailer to put humans under bondage to sin (3:22–23), and became a curse over them (3:10). Locked up in the prison house of sin, Jews under the law were essentially no different from pagans in their enslavement to the elemental spirits of the world (*stoicheia tou kosmou*, 4:1, 3).

Here Paul employs a new Exodus typology. In the fullness of time, God sent his Son, born of a woman, to redeem those under the law that they might be adopted as sons (Gal 4:4–5). Just as Israel was "redeemed" (3:13) from slavery at the time designated by God (cf. Ge 15:13) and called a "son" (Ex 4:22–23; Hos 11:1; cf. Ro 9:4), so in the eschatological fullness of time, God sent his messianic Son (2Sa 7:12, 14), in whom "all" have become sons (Gal 3:26–27).[37]

---

[35]See J. M. G. Barclay, *Obeying the Truth: Paul's Ethics in Galatians* (Minneapolis: Fortress, 1991), 36–74.

[36]Ibid., 102–5.

[37]See J. M. Scott, "Adoption, Sonship," in *DPL*, 15–18; idem, *Adoption as Sons of God: An Exegetical Investigation into the Background of* υἱοθεσία *in the Corpus Paulinum,* WUNT, vol. 2 (Tübingen: Mohr, 1992), 48. Scott points to early Judaism's expectation that God would adopt Israel, with the Messiah, as his sons (cf. Jub 1:25; TJud 24:1–4; 4QFlor 1:11; cf. also 2Co 6:18). For a study in Paul's use of the Exodus motif elsewhere, see S. C. Keesmaat, "Exodus and the Intertextual Transformation of Tradition in Romans 8.14–30," *JSNT* 54 (1994): 29–56.

The irony is that the objects of God's redemption were in bondage not to Egypt but to the law, into whose custody the first Israel was delivered. Moreover, it was by bearing the curse of this law (Gal 3:13) that Jesus Messiah brought about a new Exodus. The term Paul uses here for "redeemed" (*exagorazō*) is drawn from the slave market and not from warfare. But the new Exodus typology is plainly present, and the parallelism of thought with Paul's opening thanksgiving for redemption in Galatians 1:4–"to rescue us from the present evil age"–hints at the possibility that here too the pattern of divine warfare was influencing his thought.

In fact, Christ's taking on the curse of the covenant at the cross (Gal 3:13) suggests that Paul is alluding to more than an obscure reference to a capital penalty in Israel's law. "Hanging on a tree" (followed by burial under stones or being sealed in a cave) was a penalty meted out by Israel to the conquered kings of Canaan (Jos 8:29; 10:26). In a reversal of that imagery, Christ absorbed the eschatological judgment of the divine warrior against Israel and so brought redemption for his people. Christ died by hanging on a tree in his own land. The full force of the divine warrior's wrath was unleashed against this representative of Israel.[38] Through the cross, the eschatological in-breaking of God's judgment, there emerged a new creation (Gal 6:15). The exile and restoration of Israel were transmogrified into the death and resurrection of Christ.

Ephesians 2:14–15 is one other place where the law is cast as an enemy, and the only place where Christ is said to have "destroyed" the law. The law there is likened to a "barrier" or "dividing wall of hostility." This reference is to the law's forming a barrier (by food laws, circumcision, and observance of holy days) of racial and ethnic hostility (cf. 2:14, 16) between

---

[38]This develops an observation made by Wright in *The Climax of the Covenant*, 153, and in "Jerusalem in the New Testament" in *Jerusalem Past and Present in the Purposes of God*, ed. P. W. L. Walker (Cambridge: Tyndale House, 1992), 53–77, 64.

Jews and Gentiles,[39] thereby establishing one of the outstanding social antagonisms within the human family of the ancient Mediterranean world. The law's separating function was physically illustrated by the balustrade in the Jerusalem temple compound, an architectural barrier separating the Court of the Gentiles from the inner courts and engraved with the warning of the penalty of death for Gentiles who crossed it. The temple, being a microcosm of the world, represented the ideal geographical distinction between Israel in her land of inheritance—with Yahweh dwelling at the center—and the nations in their respective territories. This "law with its commandments and regulations" Christ "destroyed" (*katargeō*, 2:15) or "put to death" (*apokteinō*, 2:16) "in his flesh"—a shorthand allusion to his death on the cross.

The imagery perhaps pushes the divine-warrior theme to the limit—Yahweh destroys the law! But here we must consider a remarkable confluence of Old Testament themes in the space of no more than twelve verses (Eph 2:11–22). The addressees are Gentiles who were once "separate from Christ, excluded from citizenship in Israel and foreigners to the covenants of the promise" (2:12). In other words, under the old covenant, they were potential enemies of Israel; and as nations outside the land of promise (those occupying the land being automatically subject to the "ban," Dt 20:16–18), they were subject to the assault of Israel and her divine warrior if they rejected an offer of peace (20:10–15). But now they "have been brought near through the blood of Christ" (Eph 2:13), who is "our peace" (2:14).

In other words, the law, which had separated foreigners from the promise of Israel and made distant Gentiles the object of covenant curse, has been assaulted and destroyed by God's Messiah. He—not they—has been executed on the cross (cf. Dt

---

[39] *The Letter of Aristeas* 139 refers to Torah as an "impenetrable fence and iron wall."

20:13). And this Messiah has come and proclaimed peace to those "far" (i.e., Gentiles; cf. Dt 20:10) and to those "near" (i.e., Israel; cf. Isa 57:19; Eph 2:17). The result of this triumph over the law is a new creation—Paul speaks of Christ creating (*ktizō*) "one new man" (2:15)—unblemished by the old separation and hostility of Jew and Gentile. Both have "access" (*prosagōgē*, 2:18, a term used in political contexts of the right of audience with a king) to the sacred courts of the New Jerusalem, so to speak, and may come before the heavenly king. Not only does this victory issue in peace and a new creation; it is capped by the building of a new temple, with apostles and prophets the foundation, Christ the key stone, and believers its building blocks. The old pattern of divine warfare—conflict, triumph, new creation, and temple building—is recapitulated in Christ.

Ephesians 4:8–9 can be viewed as extending this story, as Paul describes how Christ has outfitted his temple-body for ministry (Eph 4:11–16). Paul recites a line from Psalm 68:18, a psalm replete with divine-warrior imagery, and applies to Christ the picture of the victorious divine warrior's ascending to his sanctuary "on high," taking "captivity captive" (KJV) in his victorious procession. But whereas in the psalm the divine warrior *receives* gifts, the victorious Christ *gives* gifts to his people. Paul may have been familiar with the Jewish interpretive tradition preserved for us in the Targum on Psalm 68:18, in which Moses is identified as the one who ascended on high to receive the Torah.[40] This line of interpretation seems to owe its origin to the use of the psalm in the Jewish observance of Pentecost, which celebrated the giving of the law to Israel. The captives in this Pauline reinterpretation seem to be the principalities and powers, who are now subject to the victorious Christ (Eph 1:20–21). The triumph and exaltation of Christ are directly related to the exercise of his sovereign purposes over the universe and the church.

---

[40]*Midr. Tᵉhillim* on Ps 68:11; Abot R. Nat. 2.2a.

♦ 10 ♦

Paul: The Holy Warriors of Christ and the Day of the Lord

Paul not only speaks of the defeat of the powers in the death and resurrection of Christ, but he also applies the theme of the divine warrior to the life of believers and the church and to the hope of a final resolution of the conflict of the ages.

SOLDIERS OF CHRIST

Within the Pauline corpus, the theme of believers engaged in divine warfare is most clearly articulated in Ephesians 6:12–17. But readers of Paul frequently overlook its presence elsewhere. In 1 Thessalonians 5:8, Paul enjoins believers to arm themselves for the warfare of God "since we belong to the day." Like disciplined soldiers, they are to "be self-controlled" and to put on "faith and love as a breastplate, and the hope of salvation as a helmet." In Romans, Paul uses this imagery twice. Believers are not to offer their bodily members to sin as weapons ("instruments," *hopla*) of wickedness, but rather offer themselves to God and their members as weapons of righteousness (Ro 6:13, 23). Later, Paul employs the night-day imagery in much the same way as in 1 Thessalonians: "The night is nearly over; the day is almost here. So let us put aside the deeds of darkness and put on the armor (*hopla*) of light" (Ro 13:12). The language seems to have much in common with Israel's apocalyptic warfare as described in the Qumran War Scroll.

Finally, pressed to defend his ministry, Paul applies this imagery to his own apostolic ministry. As one on the cutting edge of the progress of God's kingdom, he wages war "in truthful speech and in the power of God (*en dynamei theou*); with weapons (*hoplōn*) of righteousness in the right hand and in the left" (2Co 6:7). Or again,

> For though we live in the flesh, we do not wage war (*strateuometha*) as the flesh does. The weapons (*hopla*) we fight with (*tēs strateias*) are not the weapons of the flesh. On the contrary, they have divine power (*dynata tō theō*) to demolish strongholds (*ochyrōmatōn*; cf. Pr 21:22 LXX). We demolish arguments and every pretension that sets itself up against the knowledge of God, and we take captive (*aichmalotizōntes*) every thought to make it obedient to Christ. (2Co 10:3–5)[1]

To these we can add 1 Corinthians 15:32, Paul's reference to having "fought wild beasts" (*ethēriomachēsa*) at Ephesus. The likelihood is that Paul has in mind a figurative battle, possibly against his opponents. The equation between "beasts" and enemies of the kingdom of God may be found in Daniel 7 (building on animals being subject to Adam as in Ge 1–2 and Ps 8:6–8), and *Jubilees* and the *Testaments of the Twelve Patriarchs* (TNaph 8:4, 6; TJos 5:2) align Israel with Adam and the nations with the beasts (cf. Ex 23:29). Paul may have conceived of his struggle at Ephesus as against spiritual enemies.[2]

---

[1]See A. Malherbe, "Antisthenes and Odysseus and Paul at War," *HTR* 76 (1983): 143–73 for the thesis that Paul was here influenced by Greek literature.

[2]A. T. Hanson, "Militia Christi," in *The Paradox of the Cross in the Thought of St. Paul*, JSNTSup, vol. 17 (Sheffield: JSOT), 120. For Adam/Israel vs. beasts/nations see N. T. Wright, "Adam, Israel and the Messiah," in *The Climax of the Covenant* (Minneapolis: Fortress, 1992), 23–25.

Again, the theme shows through in Philippians 1:27–30, where Paul encourages the Philippians to "stand firm in one spirit, contending as one man for the faith of the gospel." They are not to be intimidated by their opponents, who will be destroyed, while true believers will be saved. This struggle entails suffering, the same struggle and suffering the Christians in Philippi have observed in Paul.

Finally, in the Pastorals, we find Paul encouraging his young "lieutenant," Timothy, to "endure hardship with us like a good soldier of Christ Jesus. No one serving as a soldier gets involved in civilian affairs—he wants to please his commanding officer" (2Ti 2:3–4). Epaphroditus and Archippus are called "fellow soldiers" (Php 2:25; Phm 2), and Paul compares his own working for a living to the improbability of someone in military service paying his own expenses (1Co 9:7). Finally, in three instances, Paul uses the term *synaichmalōtos*, "fellow prisoner of war" (Ro 16:7; Col 4:10; Phm 23), to refer to his coworkers.

These scattered echoes of the language of divine warfare, now applied to Christian discipleship and apostolic mission, give added support to our thesis that when Paul thought of Christ and his church, he drew deeply on the Old Testament archetypes of God and Israel. And when the occasion was appropriate, he could naturally speak of the church's fulfilling the role of Israel as God's army of warriors, dedicated to his kingdom and reliant on his power. But nowhere is this struggle elaborated and the enemy identified as clearly as it is in Ephesians 6.

Developing the contrast between divine warfare and that of the flesh (2Co 10:3–5), Paul points out that the enemy of the church does not consist of "flesh and blood" enemies (like those of the old Israel); God's people are now engaged with enemies in the form of principalities, powers, and "the spiritual forces of evil in the heavenly realms" (Eph 6:12). These powers are under the direction of their leader, "the devil," whose "schemes" they carry out against the church. While Israel was organized and regulated as the army of God in the desert, dependent on the victorious power of Yahweh, the church has been outfitted in spiritual weaponry and finds her strength "in the Lord and in his mighty power" (6:10).

The language and imagery employed in Ephesians 6 seem to have been refracted through Isaiah 11:4–5 and 59:17. The first of these passages speaks of the "Branch" from the "stump of Jesse" (11:1):

> He will strike the earth with the rod of his mouth;
>   with the breath of his lips he will slay the wicked.
> Righteousness will be his belt
>   and faithfulness the sash around his waist.

In Isaiah 59:17–18, Yahweh, seeing that there was no one to intervene on Israel's behalf, brought victory by his own arm:

> He put on righteousness as his breastplate,
>   and the helmet of salvation on his head;
> he put on the garments of vengeance
>   and wrapped himself in zeal as in a cloak.
> According to what they have done,
>   so will he repay
> wrath to his enemies
>   and retribution to his foes....

With the armor Isaiah attributes to God or the Son of David, Paul outfits the church as the new humanity, the new Israel, in its battle against the powers of this age. Using the armor of God, believers can find strength in the Lord to wage their spiritual battles (Eph 6:10–11; cf. v. 13). The specific attributes of the armor may also reflect the influence of Wisdom 5:17–20:

> The Lord will take his zeal as his whole armor,
>   and will arm all creation to repel his enemies;
> he will put on righteousness as a breastplate,
>   and wear impartial justice as a helmet;
> he will take holiness as an invincible shield,
>   and sharpen stern wrath for a sword
>   and creation will join with him to fight against his frenzied foes.
>   (NRSV)

Early in the letter to the Ephesians, the readers were reminded of the surpassing greatness of God's power, "the working of his mighty strength which he exerted in Christ when he raised him from the dead and seated him at his right hand," (Eph 1:19-20), far above every rule, authority, power, dominion, and "every title that can be given" in this age and in the age to come (1:21). As he did for Israel, God has now defeated the powers in a new Exodus; now God and Christ are exalted over the "gods" of this world. As with the first Adam, all things are under the Messiah's feet (Eph 1:22; cf. Ps 8:6). And what is true of Messiah, the representative head of the church, his body (the new humanity), is true also of his people (1:23): they too operate from a position of strength.

With this typology in Paul's mind (see also Eph 2:11-22), it is no surprise that he can evoke this theme in the paraenetic context of Ephesians 6. In the rhetorical style of his contemporaries, Paul recapitulates themes and terminology from earlier in his letter. The dynamic theme of God's victory in Christ is summed up in a manner that would stir his audience's imagination and arouse them to action.[3] Like Israel, the church as the new community of God is constituted as his holy army, endued with his divine and victorious power and set against an enemy whose axis of power has already been broken. Like Israel, the new people of God have gained an inheritance of blessing.

The church is given a spatial reference, the "heavenly realms," a designation that is in some ways equivalent to the "land" or territorial dimension of Judaism. Early rabbinic Judaism is known to have spiritualized the concept of land, equating it with the "world to come" (cf. *m. Sanh.* 10:1).[4] In

---

[3]See A. T. Lincoln, *Ephesians,* WBC, vol. 42 (Waco, Tex.: Word, 1990), 432-33, for the use of the rhetorical *peroratio,* or "epilogue," in Eph 6:10-20.

[4]See W. D. Davies, *The Territorial Dimension of Judaism,* 2d ed. (Minneapolis: Fortress, 1991), 53-61 for the spiritualizing or transcendentalizing of the land in Judaism, particularly in its concentrated form of a heavenly

Colossians 1:12 Paul speaks of the "inheritance of the saints," equating it with the "kingdom of the son he loves" (1:13). And Paul can elsewhere utilize the land-centered language of "inheritance" to speak of believers inheriting the kingdom of God (cf. 1Co 6:9–10; 15:50; Eph 5:5), with Abraham due to inherit not the land, but "the world" (Ro 4:13). In Ephesians, the "heavenly realms" represent the realm of spiritual blessing in which the church participates in the work of Christ, anticipating the world to come. The Spirit is the guarantee of that inheritance (Eph 1:14). And like Israel's actual experience in the land, the heavenly realms are still betwixt and between, populated by principalities and powers who, when not beholding wide-eyed the wisdom and power of God's ways with his people (Eph 3:10; cf. 1Co 4:9), oppose God's people and must be resisted (Eph 6:12).

The weapons of the church are both the defensive armor and shield (Eph 6:13–17) and the offensive "sword of the Spirit" (6:17). The power of the church militant is found "in the Lord and in his mighty power"; and while the terminology of military paraphernalia is taken from the Roman world, the archetype of warfare is clearly Israelite.

Paul, as we have seen, evokes a cluster of recognizable emblems of Judaism and the history of Israel, of which the divine warrior is a significant—and often neglected—component. Like many Jews of his day, Paul was keenly aware that the day of the Messiah was a day of catastrophic action by God. As G. Scholem strongly emphasized, "Jewish Messianism is in its origin and by its nature ... a theory of catastrophe," involving "the catastrophic and destructive nature of the redemption on the one hand and the utopianism of the content of realized Messianism on the other."[5]

Jerusalem or temple. The equation "heavenly realms = land" is particularly significant if Paul viewed the triumph of God in Christ as the restoration of Israel.

[5]G. Scholem, *The Messianic Idea in Judaism and Other Essays on Jewish Spirituality* (New York: Schocken, 1971), 7.

But for Paul, this theme was not an invitation to triumphalism. Quite the opposite. The sign of the triumph was an instrument of weakness and shame: the Cross—the paradoxical hallmark of Paul's theology. Just as in the catastrophe of Christ's cross, the pain and suffering of the world were focused on Israel and her Messiah, so the church under the sign of the cross and in the power of the Spirit shares in the tribulation of the world and creation, awaiting the final day of redemption (Ro 8:18–27). In this, the army of God follows the apostle in the campaign, "fill[ing] up ... what is still lacking in regard to Christ's afflictions" (Col 1:24). In this too she shares in the triumph. In the face of hardship, persecution, danger, and sword—facing death all day long—followers of Christ "are more than conquerors" (see Ro 8:35–37).

THE FUTURE TRIUMPH: DAY OF THE LORD

When Paul speaks of the Day of the Lord, particularly in 1 and 2 Thessalonians, the imagery of the divine warrior is unmistakable. Moreover, this material reveals a bridge from Jesus to the Pauline letters, for much of Paul's imagery seems to have been filtered through the Jesus tradition as recorded in the apocalyptic sections of the Gospels. And in terms of the chronology of Paul's letters, the Thessalonian correspondence may give us insight into an earlier period in Paul's apostolic career. These letters may be the earliest documents preserved for us from the hand of Paul and from the early church.

When Paul spoke of the return of Christ, he used a particular word: *parousia* (1Th 2:19; 3:13; 4:15; 5:23; 2Th 2:1, 8–9; 1Co 15:23). While Paul could use *parousia* to refer to the future arrival of himself or one of his coworkers (e.g., 1Co 16:17), when he uses it of the coming of Jesus, he seems to employ it in a sense well attested outside the New Testament. *Parousia* could refer to the "arrival" or "presence" of a deity, an earthly regent, or even an army.[6] Significantly, the term is also used in the *Testaments of the Twelve Patriarchs* for the eschatological coming of God and by Josephus for theophanies of Yahweh in the Old Testament.[7]

There is clear evidence that when Paul spoke of the Parousia, he had in mind the Old Testament's Day of the Lord, now seen as a Christ event. Paul borrowed directly the Old Testament language of "day of the Lord" (1Co 5:5; 1Th 5:2; 2Th 2:2) or "the/that day" (1Th 5:4; 2Th 1:10; 2Ti 1:12; 1:18; 4:8), though he frequently sharpened it Christologically, speaking of the "day of Jesus Christ" (Php 1:6), the "day of Christ" (Php 1:10; 2:16), or the "day of our Lord Jesus Christ" (1Co 1:8).

Paul does not speak of the Parousia ("coming") of the Son of Man but of Jesus Christ the Lord.[8] In these contexts he also frequently mentions God in such a way that one gains the impression that the Lord Jesus is acting as the eschatological agent of God the Father (1Th 1:10; 4:14–16; 5:9).[9] This picture is maintained in Paul's outlining of the eschatological order of events in 1 Corinthians 15:23–28, where the progression climaxes in God being "all in all." But in Titus 2:13 the expectation of "the blessed hope—the glorious appearing of our great

---

[6]See G. Braumann, "παρουσία," *NIDNTT* 2.898–901; G. A. Deissmann, *Light from the Ancient East* (1965; reprint, Grand Rapids: Baker, 1978), 369–70.

[7]See TJud 22:3 (2); TLevi 8:15 (11); *Ant.* 3 §§80, 202–3; of the heavenly army in 9 §55.

[8]The actual usage is as follows: "Jesus" (1Th 1:10; 4:14), "Christ" (1Co 15:23), "the Lord" (1Th 4:15, 17), "the Lord Jesus" (2Th 1:7, 9; 2:8), "the Lord himself" (1Th 4:16) or "his [God's] Son from heaven" (1Th 1:10). Paul also speaks of awaiting a "Savior ... Lord Jesus Christ" (Php 3:20).

[9]"His Son from heaven ... Jesus, who rescues us from the coming wrath" in 1Th 1:10 is strikingly similar to the archangelic Melchizedek of 11QMel. This figure, modeled on the priestly warrior of Ps 110:4, for whom Yahweh will "crush kings on the day of his wrath," exacts vengeance on Belial and his spirits for the sons of light. See L. W. Hurtado, *One God, One Lord* (Philadelphia: Fortress, 1988), 95–96; P. J. Kobelski, *Melchizedek and Melchiresa*, CBQMS, vol. 10 (Washington, DC: Catholic Biblical Association of America, 1981), 54.

God and Savior, Jesus Christ" transcends the distinction Paul maintains elsewhere.

All of this points to the fact that Paul thought of the future return of Christ in terms of the Old Testament expectation of an eschatological event in which Yahweh would settle the accounts of history. God would act in Christ; but the two were not to be confused, and Paul clearly viewed Jesus as an agent of this divine enterprise. But did Paul retain the picture of the divine warrior when he spoke of this day? The evidence clearly indicates that he did.

First, Paul presents us with the visual imagery of the Lord Jesus being revealed from heaven "in blazing fire with his powerful angels" (2Th 1:7) and of the Lord Jesus coming "with all his holy ones" (1Th 3:13). The notion of angels accompanying the divine warrior is found in Zechariah 14:5, where on the Day of the Lord, Yahweh will come "and all the holy ones with him"–clearly a reference to the heavenly army (cf. Dt 33:2; 1En 1:9; Jude 14). The fire imagery is well founded in the Old Testament (Ps 104:4; Isa 29:6; 30:30; Da 7:9), but may be directly attributable to the influence of Isaiah 66:15–16, a chapter of Isaiah which, as R. Aus has argued,[10] seems to have had formative influence on Paul's eschatological expression in 2 Thessalonians.

In 1 Thessalonians 4:16–17, Paul employs spatial imagery to speak of the Lord himself coming "down from heaven" and the saints who are alive being "caught up together with [the dead in Christ] in the clouds to meet the Lord in the air" (cf. 2Ki 2:11–12). The picture is that of the Lord coming to earth as the cloud-riding divine warrior. Like those who welcome the arrival of a deliverer to a city held under siege, the saints are taken up, not to depart to heaven, but–it seems–to meet him

---

[10]R. Aus, "The Relevance of Isaiah 66:7 to Revelation 12 and 2 Thessalonians 1," *ZNW* 67 (1976): 252–68. For discussion of the textual variants "fire of flame" or "flaming fire," see I. H. Marshall, *1 and 2 Thessalonians*, NCB (Grand Rapids: Eerdmans, 1983), 176–77.

and escort him on his victorious "march" to earth. This picture may be implied in Paul's use of *apantēsin* to refer to this meeting. A well-known use of this term in Greek literature refers to an official delegation going forth from a city to meet a visiting regent or dignitary and escort him into the city.[11] Paul seems to have taken a term used of a horizontal approach and applied it to vertical descent.

This theme was familiar to both the Jewish and Greco-Roman world. In the latter cultural context, as we have seen in the Roman triumphal procession, there was a long-standing tradition of greeting a conqueror or ruler outside the gates of the city, as if he were a god, and of escorting him in procession into the city with hymns and acclamations. Once within the city, the ruler or conqueror would proceed to a temple (or temples), where by ritual acts he would initiate a new era of his reign and symbolically appropriate the newly won territory.[12]

But Paul's story probably owed more to the ritual pattern embedded in the Old Testament, of Israel accompanying Yahweh's ark of the covenant and her victorious king into Jerusalem and to the temple (Ps 68:24–35; cf. Ps 24). And we can speculate that Paul may have been familiar with the tradition found in all four Gospels of Jesus' Triumphal Entry into Jerusalem amid welcoming shouts (Ps 118:25–26) befitting an eschatological deliverer and his subsequent entrance into the temple. This story may have paved the way for an application of this image to the Parousia of Jesus Christ (cf. Mt 23:39; 25:6). Even more likely, there is good evidence that Paul was indebted to a pre-Synoptic eschatological discourse of Jesus for

---

[11]E.g., Cicero of Julius Caesar in *Ad. Att.* 8.16.2; of Octavian in *Ad. Att.* 16.11.6; cf. Mt 25:6; Acts 28:15.

[12]The entrance of Alexander the Great into Jerusalem is described in these terms by Josephus, *Ant.* 11 §§332–36. See H. S. Versnel, *Triumphus* (Leiden: Brill, 1970), and for further background information P. B. Duff, "The March of the Divine Warrior and the Advent of the Greco-Roman King: Mark's Account of Jesus' Entry into Jerusalem," *JBL* 111 (1992): 55–71.

much of the eschatological teaching we find in 1 and 2 Thessalonians.[13]

Paul's description of the heavenly war cry—the "loud command" and the "voice" of the archangel—and the "trumpet call of God" (1Th 4:16) resemble the Israelite customs attested in the narrative of David's bringing the ark of the covenant into Jerusalem "with shouts and the sound of trumpets" (2Sa 6:12–15). Indeed, these aural features of the Parousia echo with the sounds of divine warfare and the coming of the divine warrior.[14] Paul links these sounds with the raising of the dead—those who have fallen asleep—as if to arouse the whole of the people of God to meet their triumphant Lord. The blast of the trumpet recurs in Paul's reference to the "last trumpet" in his instruction to the Corinthians regarding the Resurrection (1Co 15:52). There too the context is the victory of Christ—over death (1Co 15:54–57). This association of the divine warrior with resurrection was also rooted in Israel's early hymnic traditions, where the triumph of the divine warrior signaled the renewal of creation (e.g., Ps 98:4–9).[15]

The procession of the deliverer to his holy mountain and sanctuary may also be implied in Paul's picture of the coming of Jesus to overthrow the "man of lawlessness," or "the man doomed to destruction," who notably "sets himself up in God's temple, proclaiming himself to be God" (2Th 2:3–8). His rise to power is associated with "the rebellion" (2Th 2:3). Did he,

---

[13]Cf. 1Th 4:15–17 with Mk 13:26–27/Mt 24:31; 1Th 5:1–5 with Mk 13:32–33/Lk 21:24–35; 2Th 2:4–8 with Mk 13:14; 2Th 2: 8–12 with Mk 13:22. See G. R. Beasley-Murray, *Jesus and the Future* (London: Macmillan, 1954); D. Wenham, *The Rediscovery of Jesus' Eschatological Discourse* (Sheffield, JSOT, 1984); B. Witherington, *Jesus, Paul and the End of the World* (Downers Grove, Ill.: InterVarsity Press, 1992).

[14]For "loud command" and "call" generally, see Jos 6:5; Jdg 7:20; Zep 1:16; 1Mc 3:54; for the trumpet see Nu 10:9; Jos 6:5; Jdg 6:34–35; Joel 2:1; Zep 1:16; Zec 9:14; 1Mc 3:54; cf. Mt 24:31.

[15]See L. Greenspoon, "The Origin of the Idea of Resurrection," in *Traditions in Transformation: Turning Points in Biblical Faith*, ed. B. Halpern and J. D. Levenson (Winona Lake, Ind.: Eisenbrauns, 1981), 247–322.

like Gentile conquerors/rulers, have his own procession to the temple, where he laid claim to territory? About that Paul is silent. In any case, the divine warrior comes to retake his temple throne and throw out the pretender.

Jesus himself had alluded to a time when the "abomination that causes desolation" would stand "where it does not belong" (Mk 13:14; Mt 24:15). He and Paul clearly had in mind Daniel's vision of a blasphemous object of worship set in the temple by a ruler opposed to Yahweh and his people (Da 8:13; 9:27: 11:31; 12:11). And while the distant event of Antiochus' sacrilege in the temple (168 B.C.) had burned itself into Israel's historical memory (cf. 1Mc 1:54–64), for Paul and his contemporaries there was also the event just ten years previous (A.D. 39–40), when Caligula attempted–in the face of steadfast Jewish resistance–to set up his own image in the temple.[16]

Thus, the idea of a foreign power establishing an abominating idolatrous presence in the temple became a heinous symbol of the final opposition to God's purposes in history and a signal for God and his people to respond. Paul speaks of it as a personal and bodily expression of the power already at work (2Th 2:7)–much like an incarnation of Satan who stands behind every form of idolatry. This figure will one day present himself in God's temple (2:4) in a counterfeit Parousia, accompanied by Satanic signs and wonders that will lead many astray (2:9–10). But in the Parousia of the Lord Jesus, the enemy will be overthrown and destroyed (2:8).

There is an interesting resemblance between the "man of lawlessness" in 2 Thessalonians and "Belial" in 1QM. The man of lawlessness leads a powerful eschatological opposition against God as he orchestrates the great rebellion. His association with Satan may be a counterpart to the association of Belial with the sons of darkness and their leaders. This shared pool of eschatological images also shows through in Paul's de-

---

[16]Josephus, *Ant.* 18 §§55–59, 261–309.

scription of two groups of people distinguished by the last day: those of light and those of darkness. Whereas 1QM depicts an eschatological struggle between the sons of light and the sons of darkness, in 1 Thessalonians 5:1–11 Paul speaks of the church awaiting the Day of the Lord "not in darkness" but as "sons of the light and sons of the day" (1Th 5:4–5). Then, as if to transform the eschatological scenario that surfaces in 1QM, he crafts the Christian graces into military armor: "faith and love as a breastplate" (1Th 3:6) and "the hope of salvation as a helmet" (5:8). Remarkably, in the one other place where Paul speaks of darkness and light as characterizing two classes of people, he uses the images of kingdoms, inheritance (or land), and conquest (Col 1:12–13; cf. Ro 13:12).

But a difference from the Qumran conception lies in the fact that Paul does not develop any notion of eschatological warfare between the sons of light and the sons of darkness on the Day of the Lord. For Paul, the sons of light and sons of darkness are distinguished from one another only in terms of their alignment and character (1Th 5:6–8). In the final day, there will be only two sides—no neutral ground. Elsewhere in the Thessalonian correspondence, Paul implies that the sons of light suffer at the hands of the sons of darkness (1Th 1:6; 2:14–15; 3:3–4; 2Th 1:4–7; 3:2). But the sons of light persevere through suffering and temptation as they await their divine deliverer to mete out justice and wrath to their enemy (1Th 2:16; 5:3, 9; 2Th 1:6, 8–9; 2:10–12). God's people will be rescued from this wrath (1Th 1:10; 5:9), and they await the establishment of God's kingdom (1Th 2:12; 2Th 1:5). Meanwhile, a supernatural power lies behind the afflictions they suffer for the kingdom. Named "Satan" (1Th 2:18) or "the tempter" (3:5), he will ultimately inspire the great eschatological rebellion (2Th 2:9), which will seal the doom of all who follow him (2:10–12).

Christ's conquest will be by the "spirit" or "breath" (*tō pneumati*) of his mouth and by the "splendor" (*tē epiphaneia*) of his coming (2Th 2:8). Paul's reference to the "breath/spirit of his mouth" recalls the messianic conqueror's victory depicted in Isaiah 11:4, where the "shoot ... of Jesse" (11:1) will "strike the earth with the rod of his mouth; with the breath of his lips he will slay the wicked." The LXX translates the Hebrew word for "breath" as "word" (*logos*), thus suggesting the broader interpretive associations Hellenistic Judaism could bring to this passage. In exploring the meaning of *epitimaō* in the Gospels,[17] we noted how the Old Testament and Jewish texts speak of the powerful force of that which comes forth from God's lips or nostrils—whether it be a word, a blast, a torrent, or breath. This, we argued, is language that is readily and commonly employed to speak of the divine warrior. It is echoed in references to Jesus' "rebuke" of the enemy. The way was paved for its messianic application by Isaiah 11:4, which no doubt facilitated the author of 1QSb 5:24 to write of the Davidic Messiah, "that you would smite the peoples with the might of your mouth, with your scepter devastate the land, and with the breath of your lips kill the wicked."

Paul's use of the verb *anaireō* in 2 Thessalonians 2:8 also suggests the shaping influence of Isaiah 11:4. This is the only instance we have of Paul's use of this verb, and C. H. Giblin, noting other instances of Paul's use of holy war imagery in this passage, has pointed to the frequent use of *anaireō* in the LXX to translate the Hebrew *ḥerem*.[18] Paul, in using *anaireō*, undoubtedly wishes to portray Jesus as utterly destroying his enemy.

A parallel view may be observed in the destruction of the man of lawlessness by the splendor of Christ's Parousia. Here Paul employs the verb *katargeō*, which can mean "render powerless," but used in parallel with *anaireō* probably carries its

---

[17]See pp. 99–101, above.

[18]E.g., Ex 15:9; Dt 13:15; Jos 9:26; 11:12, 17; 12:1, 7; 1Sa 15:18; Isa 11:4; 27:1, 7, 8; 65:15. See C. H. Giblin, *The Threat to Faith: An Exegetical and Theological Re-examination of 2 Thess 2*, AnBib, vol. 31 (Rome: Pontifical Biblical Institute, 1967), 89–109; see especially 91, n.1.

more forceful meaning of "destroy" or "abolish." Again the imagery of divine warfare is employed: Yahweh comes to vindicate his cause on the day of battle. *Epiphaneia*, the term Paul uses to speak of this eschatological Christophany, may be found in several Septuagintal references to the Day of the Lord.[19] This term is also used of the gods in Hellenistic literature,[20] but primarily of the emperor cult or of the appearance of high officials and military forces.[21]

With this cumulative evidence that Paul viewed the Parousia of Jesus in terms of divine warfare, a fuller picture develops. Just prior to the Day of the Lord, rebellion and hostility to God will dominate and oppress the faithful. On the Day of the Lord's appearing, he will descend from heaven as an approaching deliverer. The people of God—both the dead and the living—will rush forth to meet him and escort him to earth, where in awesome power and splendor, the divine warrior will conquer his enemy and retake his temple throne. The parousia of the enemy will be shattered in the Parousia of Christ. There is no sense of a prolonged and episodic warfare as we observe in the Qumran War Scroll, where the fortunes of battle change from side to side until a final battle that breaks the tie. The victory of Christ is sudden, swift, and sure; all those who have sided with the man of lawlessness will perish. With the final rebellion overthrown and the dead raised, the Son will then hand over the kingdom to the Father:

> Then the end will come, when he hands over the kingdom
> to God the Father after he has destroyed all dominion,
> authority and power. For he must reign until he has put all
> his enemies under his feet. The last enemy to be destroyed
> is death. For he "has put everything under his feet." (1Co
> 15:24–27)

---

[19]LXX Joel 2:11; 3:4; Hab 1:7; Mal 3:22; cf. 2Mc 2:21; 3:24; 5:4; 12:22; 14:15; 3Mc 2:9; 5:8, 35, 51.

[20]See Herodotus, *Histories*, 8.37.

[21]See B. Rigaux, *Saint Paul: Les Epîtres aux Thessaloniciens* (Paris: Gabalda, 1956), 202–4.

Revelation: Visions of Divine Warfare

The book of Revelation presents the divine warrior tradition more boldly than any other New Testament writing. This is evident not only in the fact that the seer repeatedly uses the verb *nikaō*, "to conquer" (seventeen times out of its twenty-seven occurrences in the New Testament), but even more so in the rebirth of the conflict motif and the clear echoes of imagery associated with divine warfare. The apocalyptic genre is known for its rich use of mythic language, and when we read the Apocalypse of John, we come face to face with a colorful rebirth of images.[1] The presence of the divine-warrior theme has been observed by commentators and studied in some detail.[2] Our approach will be to outline its prominent features, leaving aside questions of continuing debate—particularly those of eschatological chronology.

---

[1]To borrow the title of a speculative book on Revelation by the same name: A. M. Farrer, *A Rebirth of Images* (London: Dacre, 1949).

[2]Most significantly, for a study of the presence of the ancient combat myth in Revelation, see A. Y. Collins, *The Combat Myth in the Book of Revelation*, HDR, vol. 9 (Missoula, Mont.: Scholars, 1976).

IMAGES OF THE DIVINE WARRIOR

The overture to John's development of the divine-warrior motif is found in Revelation 1:6–7. The seer first speaks in doxology of the Exodus-like redemption worked on behalf of God's people, freeing them from their sins by blood and making them, like Israel, "a kingdom of priests" (cf. Ex 19:6). The attention then shifts to the coming of the cloud rider in an echo of Daniel 7: "Look, he is coming with the clouds" (cf. Da 7; Zec 12:10). In the ensuing vision of the heavenly throne room and "one like a son of man" (Rev 1:13), the warrior appearance of this being is affirmed. Out of his mouth comes a "sharp double-edged sword" (1:16), a feature attributed to the Isaianic Servant (Isa 49:2) and later attributed to Christ in the letter to Pergamum (2:12, 16) and to the rider on the white horse (19:15, 21).

Here, as elsewhere, the theme of the divine warrior is intimately entwined with kingship. Warfare is one of the functions of a king, encompassing the establishment and maintenance of sovereign rule. In the Apocalypse of John, the revelation of God's plan for summing up history begins with the throne-room scene of chapters 4 and 5. There God's sovereignty over creation and the Lamb's worthiness to initiate the wrap-up of this age are established. The heavenly council is gathered, thunder and lightning emanate from the throne, and the question is posed: "Who is worthy to break the seals and open the scroll?" (Rev 5:2). The answer is voiced: "The Lion of the tribe of Judah" (5:5), the Davidic warrior Messiah.

When the seer looks, he sees not a lion but a Lamb with seven horns, looking as if it had been slain (Rev 5:6). The paradox of the triumph of Christ in the cross is thus summed up in visual images. The image of a lamb may be derived from the Paschal Lamb or even the image of the Servant as a slain lamb (Isa 53:7). But the horns suggest that this is a composite image, which may include an allusion to the strong warrior ram or lamb such as in the Animal Apocalypse of 1 Enoch 85–90. There the leader of the Israelite flock is a ram who symbolizes

David (1En 89:45); later, there appear horned lambs representing the Maccabees (1En 90:9).[3]

The slain Lamb will emerge in Revelation as a figure of strength and warfare. Indeed, we immediately learn that the Exodus-like deliverance we encountered in Revelation 1:6–7 was brought about by the blood of the Lamb who was slain (5:9, where the paschal imagery shows through). And the exaltation of the Lamb to the throne (5:6) is reinforced by the acclamation of song (5:12–13). As the seals are opened and the horrors of apocalyptic judgment are unleashed on the earth, we learn that this is the result of the wrath of the Lamb (6:17). Indeed, the Lamb who has conquered by his blood (5:5–6) will be engaged in warfare with ten kings but will overcome because he is "Lord of lords and King of kings" (17:14).

At the seventh trumpet (Rev 11:15–19), the seer brings us to the verge of a great battle. A turning point in cosmic sovereignty is announced from heaven. "The kingdom of the world has become the kingdom of our Lord and of his Christ, and he will reign for ever and ever" (11:15). The heavenly chorus reveals that God has begun to exercise his reign in strength and will deliver his wrath against the rebellious nations (11:17–18; cf. Ex 15:14–15; Ps 2:1–6). But the battle is only anticipated and not yet engaged. The revelation of the heavenly temple discloses yet another image of the divine warrior: the "ark of covenant" and "flashes of lightning, rumblings, peals of thunder, an earthquake and a great hailstorm" (11:19; cf. 8:5). This vision is reminiscent of Isaiah 26:21: "See, the LORD is coming out of his dwelling to punish the people of the earth for their sins." In fact, the ensuing vision of the woman and child in Revelation 12 will develop a theme found in Isaiah 26:16–27:1.[4]

---

[3]Cf. the possible Christian interpolation in TJos 19:8–9. C. H. Dodd maintained this apocalyptic tradition to be the background of the Lamb in Revelation. See Dodd, *The Interpretation of the Fourth Gospel* (London: Cambridge University Press, 1972), 236.

[4]See the discussion of "travail" later in this chapter.

The picture that unfolds in Revelation 12:1–15:4 consists of a series of seven visionary panels, each portraying some aspect of conflict with God and his people against the powers of evil. This series lies close to the center of the Apocalypse and presents the story of divine conflict and triumph in fascinating and colorful imagery. The vision of the woman, the child, and the dragon is a rebirth of the mythic conflict between a god and the dragon of chaos,[5] but it is also detailed with the familiar theme of a male—in this case, a child—who will rule, or shepherd (*poimainein*), the nations with an iron scepter (12:5; cf. Ps 2:9).

The victory over the enemy is seen on two planes: earthly and heavenly. On the earthly plane, the woman pregnant with child is faced off against the dragon. A quick succession of events follows: the child is born (with the beast waiting to devour it as soon as he emerges from the womb) and is immediately caught up to God's throne. It seems likely, as Caird and others have suggested, that the vision is not of the nativity but of the death of Christ, cast as the eschatological birth pangs issuing in the new creation of resurrection and exaltation. This not only explains the otherwise inexplicable leap from nativity to ascension, but it makes sense of the allusion to Psalm 2, which speaks of the adoption of the Son of David not at his birth but at his exaltation (cf. Ro 1:4).[6]

---

[5]A. Y. Collins, *Combat Myth*, 65–71, finds a close similarity with the Greek myth of the birth of Apollo, in which Leto, pregnant by Zeus, is pursued by the serpent-monster Python. Leto escapes with the help of the north wind (cf. the two wings of the eagle in Rev. 12:14) and is assisted by Poseidon, god of the waters (in Rev 12:15–16 there is the analogous assistance of earth swallowing the river). Finally, the twin children, Apollo and Artemis, are born and Apollo defeats Python. In Rev 12, it is God who stands behind the deliverance; in the Greek myth, it is the high god Zeus. Collins argues for a dependence of Revelation on the Leto-Python-Apollo myth, a form of the combat myth that was current and well known in western Asia Minor during the first century B.C. and A.D.

[6]See G. G. Caird, *The Revelation of St. John the Divine* (New York: Harper & Row, 1966), 149–50. This recasting of the death of Jesus fits with the tradition

On the heavenly plane, Michael and his angels engage the dragon. This boldly sets forth the theme of divine warfare. We have already commented on Jewish notions of the role of archangels, particularly Michael (with the tradition originating in Da 12:1), in eschatological warfare. Here, behind the scene of the earthly conflict—and compressed into mythic symbols of Israel, her Messiah, and the cosmic enemy—is a dimension unseen by earthly eyes. Michael and his angels are locked in combat with the dragon and his angels. "The great dragon," identified as "the devil, or Satan, who leads the whole world astray," is "hurled to the earth, and his angels with him" (Rev 12:9). This episode recalls Jesus' comment in Luke, where on the return of the seventy-two, Jesus declares in visionary terms, "I saw Satan fall like lightning from heaven" (Lk 10:18). There too it is associated with an episode of struggle and victory on the earthly plane.

For the seer, this episode in the conflict of the ages is interpreted by a loud voice from heaven: "Now have come the salvation and the power and the kingdom of our God, and the authority of his Christ" (Rev 12:10). But the angels are not the focus of this proclamation; the saints are, who did not shrink from death and "overcame [the accuser] by the blood of the Lamb and by the word of their testimony" (12:11). Yet this is not the end of the dragon; cast down to earth, he unleashes his fury. Knowing his time is short (12:12), he violently engages the woman and her offspring in war (12:17).[7] This conflict will include fearsome opponents, appearing as a beast from the sea and a beast from the earth.[8]

---

we have observed in the Synoptics, where the cross is portrayed as an episode of divine judgment. See D. C. Allison, *The End of the Ages Has Come* (Philadelphia: Fortress, 1985), 72–73.

[7]The theme of Satan's being cast down from heaven and the reality of ongoing conflict are thus found both in Luke and in Rev 12. Satan's being cast from heaven is not his ultimate defeat.

[8]See the discussion of "the enemies" later in this chapter.

In the end, the people of God, represented as 144,000,[9] will emerge victorious, standing on Mount Zion with the Lamb. The seer is depicting an army of sanctified warriors. Not only are they standing on Mount Zion, an element symbolizing their victory in securing the holy mountain; they are also described as "those who did not defile themselves with women, for they kept themselves pure" (Rev 14:4). This is not a comment on their sexual morality. Rather, like Israel's warriors of old, they have maintained ritual purity during the season of eschatological warfare (cf. Dt 23:9–10; 1Sa 21:5) and follow their general, the Lamb, wherever he goes. And like Israel before them, they have been selected from among the nations for divine service in this calling.

Again, heavenly heralds announce that "the hour of [God's] judgment has come" (Rev 14:7), and the "wine of God's fury ... has been poured full strength into the cup of his wrath" (14:10). Torment of judgment awaits those who have followed the "beast." These warnings are followed by a vision of the divine warrior as cloud rider (14:14–20). "One 'like a son of man'" is "seated on a white cloud" with "a sharp sickle in his hand." There appear to be two harvests—the first a grain harvest representing the saints, the second a vintage harvest representing divine judgment. The images of a harvest sickle and of a winepress spilling over with blood draw on metaphors of the day of the divine warrior found in Joel 3:13 (Isa 27:12) and Isaiah 63:1–3.

---

[9]The possibility that the 144,000 carries military connotations deserves further attention. In Rev 7:1–8, we learn that the number is derived by multiplying twelve tribes by 12,000 from each tribe. The Hebrew, '*elep*, "thousand," may have served as a technical term for a military unit in Israel (Nu 1; 26; Jdg 5:8; 1Sa 17:18; 1Ch 13:1) and may have been so intended in Revelation. The census list of the 144,000 recalls in some aspects the listing in Nu 1:20–46 of able-bodied male Israelites prepared for war (Rev 14:4 also implies males). The seer's list is headed by Judah, from which the Lion of 5:5 comes, an image associated with the son of David's prowess in war.

With the introduction of the "seven last plagues" (Rev 15:1) or "bowls of God's wrath" (16:1), the focus shifts again to heaven. There standing beside a sea of glass mixed with fire are the saints "who had been victorious over the beast and his image" (15:2). Their "song of Moses" and "song of the Lamb" celebrate the righteous deeds of the Lord God Almighty, who is universal king. Once again, the triumph of divine warfare is mingled with the theme of kingship. And with the subsequent pouring of the bowls, with their plagues recalling the plagues on Egypt, the wrath of God is unleashed on the earth. With the seventh bowl (16:17) and the loud voice from the throne, a cosmic cataclysm ensues. It bears the familiar images of the divine warrior: lightning, thunder, earthquake, islands and mountains fleeing, and gargantuan hailstones falling from the sky (16:17–20). Nature both convulses and fights for the divine warrior (cf. Jos 10:11–13).

The most transparent use of the divine-warrior motif in the book of Revelation is 19:11–21. The cycles of seals, trumpets, and bowls culminate in the vision of Christ, his eyes blazing with fire and his robe dipped in blood; he is mounted on a white horse. The imagery is strongly reminiscent of Isaiah 63:2–3, where the divine warrior's garments are bloodstained from waging war against Edom. The armies of heaven following Christ the warrior recall Yahweh's leading his army in battle against the historical enemies of Israel. The seer further describes Christ having a sharp sword protruding from his mouth (Rev 19:15; cf. Isa 11:4; 49:2) and ruling with an iron rod, an allusion to Psalm 2:9 (cf. Rev 12:5). He treads the winepress of the fierce wrath of God the Almighty (cf. Isa 63:3 and Joel 4:13), and his sovereign authority is symbolized in his insignia, "KING OF KINGS AND LORD OF LORDS" (Rev 19:16; cf. Dt 9:17; Da 2:17). The enemy in this case consists of the beast, the false prophet, the kings of the earth, and their armies (Rev 19:19). The beast and the prophet are captured and cast into the lake of fire, while the kings and their armies are killed by the sword from Christ's mouth. What was heralded by the angels as the "great supper of God" is, ironically (cf. the "marriage supper of the Lamb," 19:9), a sacrificial carrion feast for the unclean scavenger birds. Sacrifice and warfare are merged in a figure of judgment.[10]

The theme of conflict and victory appears in abbreviated form in the picture of the angel's coming down from heaven, seizing and binding the ancient serpent, and casting him into the Abyss for a thousand years (Rev 20:1–4). The theme of binding is reminiscent of Jesus' parable of binding the strong man. And like that parable, the binding is associated with the theme of establishing God's kingship (20:4).

But the kingship is of a limited nature (one thousand years), and the vision continues with a renewed cycle of conflict and victory. Satan is released from prison and deceives the nations, labeled as the eschatological opponents of Ezekiel 38–39, Gog and Magog. They are gathered for one last battle. In a dark parody of the children of promise, they are as numerous as the sand on the seashore (Rev 20:8). Marching across the face of the earth, they surround the camp of God's people, otherwise called "the city he loves" (20:9). Jerusalem is once again surrounded by her enemies (cf. Ps 2:1–2; 46:6; 48:4–6). A final battle is depicted in the briefest terms: "But fire came down from heaven and devoured them" (Rev 20:9). The signature of the divine warrior is unmistakable, and the final scene of combat and victory yields to a vision of God's reign established in a "new heaven and a new earth" (21:1). The seer, as if fully aware of the tradition of *yam*/sea as an archetype of cosmic evil, declares, "And there was no longer any sea" (21:1).

In the midst of a book so redolent with the theme of God's vindication of his people, it is sobering to recognize that

---

[10]Cf. the imagery of the divine warrior's eschatological battle in Isa 34:1–7 and Eze 39:17–20. The theme of birds feasting on flesh is present in both passages; Isa 34 highlights the aspect of sacrificial banquet. In Canaanite myth this is paralleled by Anat's slaying of Mot, and his remains being consumed by birds (*CTA* 6.2.31–38).

the theme of the divine warrior's fighting against his people is not absent. Early in the book, the church at Pergamum is charged with having those who "hold to the teaching of Balaam" (2:14). If they do not repent, the one like the son of man will come and fight against them with the sword of his mouth" (2:16; cf. 2:23). Here is a poignant reminder that the Lord of the second covenant is the same as the Lord of the first, zealous for the holiness of his people (and recalling the zeal of Phineas against the sin of Balaam in Nu 25).

THE ENEMIES OF THE DIVINE WARRIOR

The theme of the divine warrior is portrayed not only by echoes and images of the warrior and his warfare, but is set off against the foil of enemies. Christ as divine warrior is contrasted in various ways with the hellish warrior of Revelation 13, the beast. This beast, emerging from the sea, is described as having ten horns, seven heads, and ten diadems on his head. The seven heads find a remarkable parallel in the seven-headed dragon, *lotan* (Heb. Leviathan) of the Ugaritic texts (CTA 5.1.28; cf. Ps 74:14; Isa 27:1). The diadems are comparable to the diadems on Christ's head. The contrast is further developed in the name written on Christ, which "no one knows but he himself" and which is called "the Word of God" (Rev 19:12–13). Finally, "On his thigh he has this name written: KING OF KINGS AND LORD OF LORDS" (19:16). On each head of the opposing beastly warrior was "a blasphemous name" (13:1). The association of the beast with the cosmic enemy, Sea, is also underscored in 13:1. This is paralleled by the beast arising from the Abyss (11:7), which in the vocabulary of ancient combat myth is an equivalent to Sea.[11]

---

[11]The LXX translates Hebrew *t'hôm* with the Greek *abyssos*, and *t'hôm*, "deep," and *yam*, "sea," are used in parallel in the Old Testament (Job 28:14; Ps 33:7; Isa 51:10). See Collins, *Combat Myth*, 165–67. Cf. Da 7:2–3; 2Ba 29:4.

Satan's role is clearly a key element. He is identified as the archenemy, the dragon (Rev 12:9), who sought to vanquish the male child (12:4) and is furiously intent on warfare against the saints (12:17). This he carries out either directly with his angels (12:7) or by his chief surrogates, the two beasts (13:7, 11–13). The enemy is presented as having both a satanic and a human face. This may be observed in the similar descriptions of both the beast arising from the sea in chapter 13 and the scarlet beast of chapter 17.[12]

The sixth and seventh bowl visions depict the build-up and execution of warfare. Three frog-like spirits emerge from the mouth of the dragon and the false prophet. These spirits, able to perform miraculous signs, gather the kings of the earth for battle "on the great day of God Almighty" (Rev 16:13–14; cf. the lying spirits who incite warfare in 1Ki 22:21–23). The scene of this earthly battle is set as the kings are gathered at "Armageddon" (Rev 16:16). The feature of earthly kings organized for battle appears later in two visionary panels—as making war with the beast against the rider on the white horse (19:19), and as Gog and Magog, mustered by Satan to march against the camp of God's people (20:7–9).

THE TRAVAIL AND OUTCOME OF DIVINE WARFARE

As we have noted repeatedly, divine warfare brings travail. This too is evident in Revelation. Early in the Apocalypse, at the coming of the cloud rider, those who pierced him and all the peoples of the earth, see him and mourn (Rev 1:7; cf. Zec 12:10; Mt 24:30). At the sixth seal (Rev 6:12–17), the great day of the wrath of the Lamb, the creation convulses and writhes in tribulation, led by the heavenly bodies as the sun darkens, the

---

[12]For comparison, see Collins, *Combat Myth*, 171–72, who identifies the beast with Rome, reaching its zenith as an adversary in Nero.

moon turns to blood (cf. 8:12), and stars fall from the sky like figs shaken from a tree. Humankind, led by the princes and generals, flees to the craggy mountains to escape the wrath of the Lamb. The travail of the people of God is seen in the vision of the woman, the child, and the dragon (12:1–17). The woman, representing the people of God (cf. Israel or Zion as a woman in passages such as Isa 1:8; 3:16–17; 4:4; 16:1; 37:22; 47:1; 52:2; 62:11; 66:8), gives birth to the child-messiah in painful labor, symbolizing the eschatological tribulation associated with the Day of the Lord, here more particularly seen as the "messianic woes."

Behind this drama lies Isaiah 26:16–27:1, where Israel—under divine discipline—writhes in labor but gives birth only to wind, not salvation. But Yahweh will bring salvation, raising Israel from the dust, like the earth giving birth to its dead. Meanwhile, Israel must hide until the wrath of Yahweh has passed, for the divine warrior is coming from his heavenly temple and will punish the earth for its sins. For Isaiah, "that day" will find the Lord punishing the great serpent and monster of the sea, Leviathan (Isa 27:1). For the seer of Revelation, Leviathan is the enormous red dragon (Rev 12:3–4), "that ancient serpent called the devil, or Satan, who leads the whole world astray" (12:9). The dragon's pursuit of the woman brings suffering on the rest of her offspring as they are pursued and attacked (12:17), even though his time is limited and "short" (12:12). These may also be the conditions under which the seven churches are encouraged to prevail against the forces of evil.[13] The Apocalypse as a whole underscores the tribulation and martyrdom of the saints as their lot during the period conflict.[14]

If the theme of nature's and humanity's languishing and suffering during the season of war is clearly evident, so is the

---

[13]Note the theme of "overcoming" (*nikaō*) in 2:7, 11, 17, 26; 3:5, 12, 21; 15:2.

[14]E.g., 2:3, 10, 13, 24–25; 3:4, 10; 6:9–11; 7:14.

theme of nature's breaking forth with new vitality when the divine warrior triumphs. In Revelation 20, the earth and sky flee from the presence of the divine warrior as he presides on the great white throne to render judgment (20:11). After the judgment and the annihilation of death and Hades in the lake of fire (20:14), "a new heaven and a new earth" and a "new Jerusalem" appear (21:1–2). And, echoing the divine warrior's victory over *yam* (the sea), there is no longer any sea (21:1). In the new creation, there is no death, pain, tears, or mourning (21:4); the old order has passed away and all things are new (21:4–5). Within the city flows a river of life from beneath the throne of God (22:1).

As we saw in chapter 2, the victory of the divine warrior is celebrated by song, particularly what is called a "new song." When the divine warrior goes forth to fight, creation languishes and music stops. But with his triumph, creation is rejuvenated and music breaks forth. It is notable that some of the outstanding songs embedded in the narrative of the Old Testament are songs of divine victory—the Song of Moses (Ex 15), the Song of Deborah (Jdg 5), and David's song in 2 Samuel 22 (= Ps 18). The term "new song" occurs also in Revelation 5:9 and 14:3, and in both cases the ethos of divine warfare is close at hand. In Revelation 5, the words of the song are recited (5:9–10) and celebrate the worthiness of the slain but reigning Lamb, who will open the seals and initiate the eschatological warfare. In Revelation 14, the song is sung by the 144,000 on Mount Zion who, like holy warriors, "follow the Lamb wherever he goes" (14:4).

Two themes related to the pattern of divine warfare—kingship and temple building—are developed along fresh lines. The vision of the enthroned Christ in Revelation 20:4–6 is followed by the establishment of the royal city, the Holy City, Jerusalem, coming down from heaven (21:10). When the city is measured, it is found to have no temple, for "the Lord God Almighty and the Lamb are its temple" (21:22). Here again, the transcendent nature of the eschatological triumph of God and the new order are depicted by manipulating the traditional symbols. The final chapter is the assertion of the universal sovereignty of the heavenly king and an overflowing of *shalom*. Divine warfare has achieved its goal in the peace of the new heaven and new earth.

◆ Bibliography ◆

Ackroyd, P. *Exile and Restoration*. OTL. Philadelphia: Westminster, 1968.

Allison, D. C. *The End of the Ages Has Come*. Philadelphia: Fortress, 1985.

Alter, R. *The Art of Biblical Narrative*. New York: Basic Books, 1981.

Anderson, B. W. *Creation Versus Chaos: The Reinterpretation of Mythical Symbolism in the Bible*. New York: Association Press, 1967.

Arnold, C. E. *Ephesians: Power and Magic. The Concept of Power in Ephesians*. SNTSMS, vol. 63. Cambridge: Cambridge Univ. Press, 1989.

_____. *Powers of Darkness: Principalities and Power in Paul's Letters*. Downers Grove, Ill.: InterVarsity Press, 1992.

Auerbach, E. *Mimesis*. Princeton, N.J.: Princeton Univ. Press, 1953.

Aus, R. "The Relevance of Isaiah 66:7 to Revelation 12 and 2 Thessalonians 1." *ZNW* 67 (1976): 252–68.

Balchin, J. F., D. H. Field, and T. Longman III. *The Complete Bible Study Tool Kit*. Downers Grove, Ill.: InterVarsity Press, 1991.

Barclay, J. M. G. *Obeying the Truth: Paul's Ethics in Galatians*. Minneapolis: Fortress, 1991.

Barnett, P. W. "The Jewish Sign Prophets—A.D. 40–70: Their Intentions and Origin." *NTS* 27 (1981): 679–97.

Barrett, C. K. *The Holy Spirit and the Gospel Tradition*. London: SPCK, 1970.

Barton, J. *Reading the Old Testament*. Philadelphia: Westminster, 1984.

Baumann, G. "παρουσία." In *The New International Dictionary of New Testament Theology*, 2.898–901. Ed. C. Brown. Grand Rapids: Zondervan, 1976.

Beker, J. C. *Paul the Apostle: The Triumph of God in Life and Thought*. Philadelphia: Fortress, 1980.

Berkhof, H. *Christ and the Powers*. Scottdale, Pa.: Herald, 1977.

Best, E. *Following Jesus: Discipleship in the Gospel of Mark.* JSNTSup, vol 4. Sheffield: JSOT, 1981.

Betz, O. "Jesu Heiliger Krieg." *NovT* 2 (1957): 116–37.

Black , M. "πᾶσαι ἐξουσίαι αὐτῷ ὁποταγήσονται." In *Paul and Paulinism,* 74–82. Ed. M. D. Hooker and S. G. Wilson. London: SPCK, 1982.

Boer, M. C. de. *The Defeat of Death.* JSNTSup, vol. 22. Sheffield: JSOT, 1988.

Borg, M. J. *Conflict, Holiness and Politics in the Teachings of Jesus.* New York: Edwin Mellen, 1984.

Bronner, L. *The Stories of Elijah and Elisha as Polemics against Baal Worship.* Leiden: Brill, 1968.

Buchanan, G. W. "Mark 11,15–19: Brigands in the Temple." *HUCA* 30 (1959): 169–77.

Caird, G. B. *Principalities and Powers.* Oxford: Clarendon, 1956.

———. *The Revelation of St. John the Divine.* New York: Harper & Row, 1966.

———. *Paul's Letters from Prison.* Oxford: Oxford Univ. Press, 1976.

Calvin, J. *Commentaries on the Four Last Books of Moses.* Vol. 1. Trans. C. W. Bingham. Grand Rapids: Baker, 1981.

Campbell, A. F. *The Ark Narrative.* SBLDS, vol. 16. Missoula, Mont.: Scholars, 1975.

Carmignac, J. "Que'est-ce que l'Apocalyptique? Son emploi à Qumran." *RevQ* 37 (1979): 3–33.

Childs, B. S. *Introduction to the Old Testament as Scripture.* Philadelphia: Fortress, 1979.

Christ, C. P. "Feminist Liberation Theology and Yahweh as Holy Warrior: An Analysis of Symbol." In *Women's Spirit Bonding.* Ed. J. Kalven and M. I Buckley, 202–12. New York: Pilgrim, 1984.

Christensen, D. L. *Transformations of the War Oracle in Old Testament Prophecy.* HDR Missoula, Mont.: Scholars, 1975.

Collins, A. Y. *The Combat Myth in the Book of Revelation.* HDR, vol. 9. Missoula, Mont.: Scholars, 1976.

Collins, J. J. "The Mythology of Holy War in Daniel and the Qumran War Scroll: A Point of Transition in Jewish Apocalyptic." *VT* 25 (1975): 596–612.

———, ed. *Apocalypse: The Morphology of a Genre.* Semeia, vol. 14. Missoula, Mont.: Scholars, 1979.

_____. "Messianism in the Maccabean Period." In *Judaisms and Their Messiahs at the Turn of the Christian Era*, 97–109. Ed. J. Neusner, et al. Cambridge: Cambridge Univ. Press, 1987.

Conrad, E. W. *Fear Not Warrior: A Study of the* 'al tira' *Pericopes in the Hebrew Scriptures*. BJS, vol. 75. Chico, Calif.: Scholars, 1985.

Conzelmann, H. *The Theology of St. Luke*. New York: Harper, 1961.

Coogan, M. D. *Stories from Ancient Canaan*. Philadelphia: Westminster, 1978.

Craigie, P. C. "Yahweh Is A Man of Wars." *SJT* 22 (1969): 183–88.

_____. "Psalm XXIX in the Hebrew Poetic Tradition." *VT* 22 (1972): 143–51.

_____. *The Problem of War in the Old Testament*. Grand Rapids: Eerdmans, 1978.

Cross, F. C. "Notes on a Canaanite Psalm in the Old Testament." *BASOR* 117 (195): 19–21.

_____. *Canaanite Myth and Hebrew Epic*. Cambridge: Harvard Univ. Press, 1973.

Curtis, A. H. W. "The Subjugation of the Waters' Motif in the Psalms: Imagery or Polemic?" *JSS* 23 (1978): 244–56.

Davies, W. D. *The Territorial Dimension of Judaism*. 2d ed. Minneapolis: Fortress, 1991.

Day, J. *God's Conflict with the Dragon and the Sea*. Cambridge: Cambridge Univ. Press, 1975.

Delling, G. "στοιχεῖον." In *The Theological Dictionary of the New Testament*, 7.670–83. Ed. G. Kittel, et al. Trans. G. Bromiley. Grand Rapids: Eerdmans, 1964–76.

Derrett, J. D. M. "Contributions to the Study of the Gerasene Demoniac." *JSNT* 3 (1979): 2–17.

Dibelius, M. *Die Geisterwelt im Glauben des Paulus*. Gottingen: Vandenhoeck and Ruprecht, 1909.

Dodd, C. H. *The Interpretation of the Fourth Gospel*. London: Cambridge Univ. Press, 1972.

Duff, P. B. "The March of the Divine Warrior and the Advent of the Greco-Roman King: Mark's Account of Jesus' Entry into Jerusalem." *JBL* 111 (1992): 55–71.

Dunn, J. D. G. *Jesus and the Spirit*. Philadelphia: Westminster, 1975.

Egan, R. B. "Lexical Evidence on Two Pauline Passages." *NovT* 19 (1977): 34–62.

Eller, V. *War and Peace from Genesis to Revelation.* Scottdale, Pa.: Herald, 1981.

Evans, C. A. "Paul and the Hermeneutics of 'True Prophecy': A Study of Romans 9–11." *Biblica* 65 (1984): 560–570.

_____. "Prophet, Paul as." In *Dictionary of Paul and His Letters,* 762–65. Ed. G. F. Hawthorne, et al. Downers Grove, Ill.: InterVarsity Press, 1993.

Farrer, A. M. *A Rebirth of Images.* London: Dacre, 1949.

_____. *St. Matthew and St. Mark.* 2d. ed. Philadelphia: Westminster, 1966.

Fee, G. D. *New Testament Exegesis: A Handbook for Students and Pastors.* Philadelphia: Westminster, 1983.

_____. *The First Epistle to the Corinthians.* NICNT. Grand Rapids: Eerdmans, 1987.

Fish, T. "War and Religion in Ancient Mesoptamia." *BJRL* 23 (1939): 387–402.

Fitzmyer, J. *The Gospel According to Luke.* 2 vols. AB. Garden City, N.Y.: Doubleday, 1981–85.

Forsyth, N. *The Old Enemy: Satan and the Combat Myth.* Princeton, N.J.: Princeton Univ. Press, 1987.

Fredricksson, H. *Jahwe als Krieger: Studien zum alttestamentlichen Gottesbild.* Lund: C. W. K. Gleerup, 1945.

Freedman, D. N. *Pottery, Poetry, and Prophecy.* Winona Lake, Ind.: Eisenbrauns, 1980.

Gaffin, R. B. "The New Testament as Canon." In *Inerrancy and Hermeneutic,* 165–83. Ed. H. M. Conn. Grand Rapids: Baker, 1988.

Garrett, S. R. "Exodus from Bondage: Luke 9:31 and Acts 12:1–24." *CBQ* 52 (1990): 656–80.

_____. *The Demise of the Devil.* Minneapolis: Augsburg Fortress, 1989.

Geller, S. A. "The Language of Imagery in Psalm 114." In *Lingering Over Words,* 179–94. Ed. T. Abusch et al. Winona Lake, Ind.: Eisenbrauns, 1990.

Giblin, C. H. *The Threat to Faith: An Exegetical and Theological Re-examination of 2 Thess 2.* AnBib, vol. 31. Rome: Pontifical Biblical Institute, 1967.

Ginsberg, H. L. "A Phoenician Hymn in the Psalter." *XIX Congresso Internationale degli Orientalisti.* Rome, 1935.

Goldingay, J. E. *Daniel.* WBC. Waco, Tex.: Word, 1989.

Goldstein, J. A. "How the Authors of 1 and 2 Maccabees Treated the 'Messianic' Promises." In *Judaisms and Their Messiahs at the Turn of the Christian Era,* 69–96. Ed. J. Neusner, et al. Cambridge: Cambridge Univ. Press, 1987.

Good, R. M. "The Just War in Ancient Israel." *JBL* 104 (1985): 385–400.

Gottwald, N. K. "Holy War." In *The Interpreter's Dictionary of the Bible Supplement (IDBSup),* 942–44. Ed. K. R. Crim. Nashville: Abingdon, 1976.

Green, J. B. "Jesus and the Daughter of Abraham (Luke 13:10–17): Test Case for a Lucan Perspective on Jesus' Miracles." *CBQ* 51 (1989): 643–54.

Greenspoon, L. J. "The Origin of the Idea of Resurrection." In *Traditions in Transformation,* 247–321. Ed. B. Halperin and J. D. Levenson. Winona Lake, Ind.: Eisenbrauns, 1981.

Guelich, R. A. *Mark 1–8:26.* WBC, vol. 34A. Dallas: Word, 1989.

Gurney, R. J. M. *God in Control: An Exposition of the Prophecies of Daniel.* West Sussex, Eng.: Walter, 1980.

Hafemann, S. J. *Suffering and Ministry in the Spirit: Paul's Defense of His Ministry in II Corinithians 2:14–3:3.* Grand Rapids: Eerdmans, 1990.

Hanson, A. T. "Militia Christi." In *The Paradox of the Cross in the Thought of St. Paul,* 99–128. Ed. A. T. Hanson. JSNTSup, vol. 17. Sheffield: JSOT, 1987.

Hanson, P. D. *The Dawn of Apocalyptic.* Philadelphia: Fortress, 1975.

_____. "Apocalypse, Genre." *IDBSup,* 27–34. Ed. K. R. Crim. Nashville: Abingdon, 1976.

_____. "Apocalypticism." *IDBSup,* 28–34. Ed. K. R. Crim. Nashville: Abingdon, 1976.

Haran, M. *Temples and Temple-Service in Ancient Israel.* Oxford: Clarendon, 1978.

Harmand, J. *La Guerre Antique de Sumer à Rome.* Presses Universitaires de France, 1973.

Hillers, D. R. *Lamentations.* AB. Garden City, N.Y.: Doubleday, 1972.

Hillmann, R. *Wasser und Berg Kosmische Vrebindungslinien zwischen dem kanaanaischen Wettergott unter Jahwe.* Halle, 1965.

Hobbs, E. C. "The Gospel of Mark and the Exodus." Ph.D. diss., University of Chicago, 1958.

Hoekema, A. *The Bible and the Future*. Grand Rapids: Eerdmans, 1979.

Hoffmann, Y. "The Day of the Lord as a Concept and a Term in the Prophetic Literature." *ZAW* 93 (1981): 37–50.

Hubbard, D. A. *Hosea*. TOTC. Downers Grove, Ill.: InterVarsity Press, 1989.

Hull, J. M. *Hellenistic Magic and the Synoptic Tradition*. SBT, vol. 28. Naperville, Ill.: Allenson, 1974.

Hultgren, A. J. *Jesus and His Adversaries*. Minneapolis: Augsburg, 1979.

Hurtado, L. W. *One God, One Lord*. Philadelphia: Fortress, 1988.

Jacobsen, T. "The Battle Between Marduk and Tiamat." *JAOS* 88 (1968): 104–8.

Jeremias, Joachim. *Jesus' Promise to the Nations*. Naperville, Ill.: Allenson, 1958.

_____. *Die Briefe an Timotheus und Titus*. Gottingen: Vandenhoeck and Ruprecht, 1963.

Jeremias, Jorg. *Theophanie. Die Geschichte einer alttestamentlichen Gattung*. Neukirchen-Vluyn, 1965.

Jones, G. H. "'Holy War' or 'Yahweh War'?" *VT* 25 (1975): 642–58.

_____. "The Concept of Holy War." In T*he World of the Old Testament*, 299–322. Ed. R. E. Clements. Cambridge: Cambridge Univ. Press, 1989.

Kang, S.-M. *Divine War in the Old Testament and in the Ancient Near East*. New York: Walter de Gruyter, 1989.

Kee, H. C. "The Terminology of Mark's Exorcism Stories." *NTS* 14 (1968): 232–46.

Keesmaat, S. C. "Exodus and the Intertextual Transformation of Tradition in Romans 8.14–30." *JSNT* 54 (1994): 29–56.

Kelber, W. *Mark's Story of Jesus*. Philadelphia: Fortress, 1979.

_____. "Kingdom and Parousia in the Gospel of Mark." Ph.D. Diss., University of Chicago, 1970.

Kennedy, J. M. "The Root *gʿr* in the Light of Semantic Analysis." *JBL* 106 (1987): 47–64.

Kim, S. *The Origin of Paul's Gospel*. Grand Rapids: Eerdmans, 1982.

Kline, M. G. *Treaty of the Great King*. Grand Rapids: Eerdmans, 1963.

_____. *The Structure of Biblical Authority*. Grand Rapids: Eerdmans, 1972.

Kloos, C. *Yhwh's Combat with the Sea: A Canaanite Tradition in the Religion of Ancient Israel*. Leiden: Brill, 1986.

_____. "The Flood on Speaking Terms with God." *ZAW* 94 (1982): 639–42.

Kobelski, P. J. *Milchizedek and Melchiresa'*. CBQMS, vol. 10. Washington, D.C.: The Catholic Biblical Association of America, 1981.

Kristeva, J. *Semiotike: Recherches pour une semanalyse*. Paris: Seuil, 1969.

Kugel, J. L. *The Idea of Biblical Poetry*. New Haven: Yale Univ. Press, 1981.

Lambert, W. G. "The Great Battle of the Mesopotamian Religious Year. The Conflict in the Akitu House." *Iraq* 25 (1969): 189–90.

Lane, W. L. *The Gospel According to Mark*. Grand Rapids: Eerdmans, 1974.

Lee, J. Y. "Interpreting the Powers in Pauline Thought." *NovT* 12 (1970): 54–69.

Leivestad, R. *Christ the Conqueror*. London: SPCK, 1954.

Lightfoot, J. B. *St. Paul's Epistles to the Colossians and to Philemon*. London, 1879.

Lightfoot, R. H. *The Gospel Message of St. Mark*. Cambridge: Cambridge Univ. Press, 1950.

Lilley, J. P. U. "Understanding the Herem." *TynB* 44 (1993): 169–77.

Lincoln, A. T. *Ephesians*. WBC, vol. 42. Waco, Tex.: Word, 1990.

Lind, M. C. *Yahweh is a Warrior*. Scottdale, Pa.: Herald, 1980.

Lohse, E. *Colossians and Philemon*. Hermeneia. Philadelphia: Fortress, 1971.

Longman III, T. "The Divine Warrior: The New Testament Use of an Old Testament Motif." *WTJ* 44 (1982): 290–307.

_____. "Psalm 98: A Divine Warrior Victory Song." *JETS* 27 (1984): 267–74.

_____. "The Form and Message of Nahum: Preaching from a Prophet of Doom." *RTJ* 1 (1985): 13–24.

_____. *Literary Approaches to Biblical Interpretation*. Grand Rapids: Zondervan, 1987.

_____. *How to Read the Psalms*. Downers Grove, Ill.: InterVarsity Press, 1988.

_____. "What I Mean by Historical-Grammatical Exegesis–Why I am Not a Literalist." *Grace ThJ* 11 (1990): 137–55.

_____. *Fictional Akkadian Autobiography.* Winona Lake, Ind.: Eisenbrauns, 1991.

_____. "Nahum." In *The Minor Prophets: An Exegetical and Expository Commentary,* vol 2. Ed. T. E. McComiskey. Grand Rapids: Baker, 1993.

Lücke, F. *Versuch einer vollständigen Einleitung in die Offenbarung Johannis und die gesammte apokalyptische Litteratur.* Bonn: E. Weber, 1832.

Luyster, R. "Wind and Water: Cosmological Symbolism in the Old Testament." *ZAW* 93 (1981): 1–10.

Macgregor, G. H. C. "Principalities and Powers: The Cosmic Background of Paul's Thought." *NTS* 1 (1954–55): 17–28.

Malherbe, A. "Antisthenes and Odysseus and Paul at War." *HTR* 76 (1983): 143–73.

Mann, T. W. *Divine Presence and Guidance in Israelite Tradition: The Typology of Exaltation.* Baltimore: Johns Hopkins Univ. Press, 1977.

Marcus, J. "Entering into the Kingly Power of God." *JBL* 107 (1988): 663–75.

_____. "The Gates of Hades and the Keys of the Kingdom (Matt. 16:18–19)." *CBQ* 50 (1988): 443–55.

_____. *The Way of the Lord: Christological Exegesis of the Old Testament in the Gospel of Mark.* Louisville: Westminster/John Knox, 1992.

Marshall, I. H. *1 and 2 Thessalonians.* NCB. Grand Rapids: Eerdmans, 1983.

_____. *The Origins of New Testament Christology.* Rev. ed. Downers Grove, Ill.: InterVarsity Press, 1991.

Martin, R. P. "Salvation and Discipleship in Luke's Gospel." In *Interpreting the Gospels,* 214–30. Ed. J. L. Mays. Philadelphia: Fortress, 1981.

_____. *Colossians: The Church's Lord and the Christian's Liberty.* London: Paternoster, 1972.

_____. *Colossians and Philemon.* 3d ed. NCB. Grand Rapids: Eerdmans, 1981.

Mauser, U. *Christ in the Wilderness.* SBT, vol. 21. Naperville, Ill.: Allenson, 1957.

Mattill, Jr., A. J. *Luke and the Last Things.* Dillsboro, N.C.: Western North Carolina Press, 1979.

McComiskey, T. E. *The Covenants of Promise: A Theology of the Old Testament Covenants.* Grand Rapids: Baker, 1985.

McCurley, F. R. *Ancient Myths and Biblical Faith: Scriptural Transformations.* Philadelphia: Fortress, 1983.

Meyer, F. de "*kbd* comme nom divine en eblaite, ougaritique et hebreu." *RThL* 11 (1980): 225–28.

Meyers, C. L. *The Tabernacle Menorah.* ASOR. Missoula, Mont.: Scholars, 1976.

Millar, W. R. *Isaiah 24–27 and the Origin of Apocalyptic.* HSM, vol. 11. Missoula, Mont.: Scholars Press, 1976.

Miller, P. D., Jr. "Fire in the Mythology of Canaan and Israel." *CBQ* 27 (1965): 256–61.

____. "The Divine Council and the Prophetic Call to War." *VT* 18 (1968): 100–107.

____. *The Divine Warrior in Early Israel.* HSM, vol. 5. Cambridge: Harvard Univ. Press, 1973.

Moran, W. L. "The End of the Unholy War and the Anti-Exodus." *Bib* 44 (1963): 333–342.

Moule, C. F. D. *The Epistles to the Colossians and to Philemon.* CGTC. Cambridge: Cambridge Univ. Press, 1957.

Mowinckel, S. *He That Cometh.* Oxford: Basil Blackwell, 1956.

Mullen, E. Th. *The Divine Council in Canaanite and Early Hebrew Literature: The Assembly of the Gods.* HSM. Missoula, Mont.: Scholars, 1980.

Murray, J. "Systematic Theology: Second Article." *WTJ* 26 (1963): 33–46.

Nickelsburg, G. W. E. "Salvation without and with a Messiah: Developing Beliefs in Writings Ascribed to Enoch." In *Judaisms and Their Messiahs at the Turn of the Christian Era.* Ed. J. Neusner et al. Cambridge: Cambridge Univ. Press, 1987.

O'Brien, P. T. *Colossians, Philemon.* WBC, vol. 44. Waco, Tex.: Word, 1982.

____. "Principalities and Powers: Opponents of the Church." In *Biblical Interpretation and the Church*, 110–50. Ed. D. A. Carson. Nashville: Thomas Nelson, 1984.

Pimentel, P. "The 'unclean spirits' of St. Mark's Gospel." *ExpT* 99 (1988): 173–75.

Pope, M. H. *El in the Ugaritic Texts.* VTS, vol. 2. Leiden: Brill, 1955.

Poythress, V. S. *Symphonic Theology.* Grand Rapids: Zondervan, 1987.

Rad, G. von. *Holy War in Ancient Israel.* 1958. Reprint, Grand Rapids: Eerdmans, 1991.

_____. "The Origin of the Concept of the Day of Yahweh." *JSS* 4 (1959): 97–108.

Reid, D. "The Christus Victor Motif in Paul's Theology." Ph.D. diss., Fuller Theological Seminary, 1982.

_____. "Principalities and Powers" and "Triumph." In *Dictionary of Paul and His Letters,* 746–52. Ed. G. F. Hawthorne, et al. Downers Grove, Ill.: InterVarsity Press Press, 1993.

Rigaux, B. *Saint Paul: Les Epîtres aux Thessaloniciens.* Paris: Gabalda, 1956.

Robertson, O. P. *The Christ of the Covenants.* Phillipsburg, N.J.: Presbyterian and Reformed, 1980.

Robinson, J. A. T. *The Body: A Study in Pauline Theology.* SBT, vol. 5. London: SCM, 1952.

Robinson, J. M. *The Problem of History in Mark.* SBT, vol. 21. Naperville, Ill.: Allenson, 1957.

Rowland, C. *The Open Heaven.* New York: Crossroad, 1982.

Rowley, H. H. *Darius the Mede and the Four World Empires in the Book of Daniel.* Cardiff: University of Wales Press Board, 1935.

Sanders, E. P. *Paul and Palestinian Judaism.* Philadelphia: Fortress, 1977.

Sandnes, K. O. *Paul—One of the Prophets? A Contribution to the Apostle's Self-Understanding.* WUNT, vol. 2:43. Tübingen: J. C. B. Mohr, 1991.

Schlier, H. *Principalities and Powers in the New Testament.* Freiburg: Herder, 1961.

Schmidt, H. H. "Heilige Krieg und Gottesfrieden im alten Testament." In *Altorientalische Welt in der alttestamentlichen Theologie,* 91–120. Ed. H. H. Schmidt. Zurich: Theologischer Verlag, 1972.

Scholem, G. *The Messianic Idea in Judaism and Other Essays on Jewish Spirituality.* New York: Schocken, 1971.

Schwally, F. *Der heilige Krieg im alten Israel.* Leipzig: Deiterich, 1901.

Schweizer, E. *The Letter to the Colossians.* Minneapolis: Augsburg, 1982.

Scott, C. A. A. *Christianity According to St. Paul.* Cambridge: Cambridge Univ. Press, 1961.

Scott, J. M. *Adoption as Sons of God: An Exegetical Investigation into the Background of* υἰοθεσία *in the Corpus Paulinum.* WUNT, vol. 2:48. Tubingen: J. C. B. Mohr, 1992.

_____. "Restoration of Israel." In *Dictionary of Paul and His Letters,* 796–805. Ed. G. F. Hawthorne, et al. Downers Grove, Ill.: InterVarsity Press, 1993.

_____. "Adoption, Sonship." In *Dictionary of Paul and His Letters,* 15–18. Ed. G. F. Hawthorne, et al. Downers Grove, Ill.: InterVarsity Press, 1993.

Segal, A. *Paul the Convert.* New Haven: Yale Univ. Press, 1990.

Smend, R. *Yahweh War and Tribal Confederation.* Nashville: Abingdon, 1970.

Smith, M. S. *The Early History of God: Yahweh and the Other Deities in Ancient Israel.* Harper & Row, 1990.

Soggin, J. A. "The Prophets on Holy War as Judgement against Israel." In *Old Testament and Oriental Studies.* Ed. J. A. Soggin, 67–81. BiOr vol. 29. Rome: Pontifical Biblical Institute, 1975.

Stern, P. D. *The Biblical Herem: A Window on Israel's Religious Experience.* BJS, vol. 211. Atlanta: Scholars Press, 1991.

Stewart, J. S. "On a Neglected Emphasis in New Testament Theology." *SJT* 4 (1951): 292–301.

Stevens, B. A. "Jesus as the Divine Warrior." *ExpT* 94 (1982–1983): 326–29.

Stolz, F. *Jahwes und Israels Krieg: Kriegstheorien und Kriegserfahrungen im Glauben des alten Israel.* Zurich: Theologischer Verlag, 1972.

Stowers, S. K. "Friends and Enemies in the Politics of Heaven: Reading Theology in Philippians," in *Pauline Theology.* Vol. 1, *Thessalonians, Philippians, Galatians, Philemon,* 105–21. Ed. by J. M. Bassler. Minneapolis: Fortress, 1981.

Stuart, D. "The Sovereign's Day of Conquest." *BASOR* 221 (1976): 159–64.

Swartley, W. *Israel's Scripture Traditions and the Synoptic Gospels: Story Shaping Story.* Peabody, Mass.: Hendrickson, 1994.

Terrien, S. L. *The Elusive Presence: Toward a New Biblical Theology.* Harper & Row, 1978.

Theissen, G. *The Miracle Stories of the Early Christian Tradition.* Philadelphia: Fortress, 1983.

Toombs, L. E. "Ideas of War." In *Interpreter's Dictionary of the Bible,* 4.796–801. Ed. G. A. Buttrick. Nashville; Abingdon, 1962.

Twelftree, G. *Christ Triumphant.* London: Hodder and Stoughton, 1985.

_____. *Jesus the Exorcist.* WUNT 2.54. Tübingen: J. C. B. Mohr (Paul Siebeck), 1993.

VanGemeren, W. *The Progress of Redemption: The Story of Salvation from Creation to the New Jerusalem.* Grand Rapids: Zondervan, 1988.

Vannoy, J. R. *Covenant Renewal at Gilgal.* Cherry Hill, N.J.: Mack, 1977.

Versnel, S. *Triumphus.* Leiden: Brill, 1970.

Vos, G. *Biblical Theology.* Grand Rapids: Eerdmans, 1948.

Wakeman, M. K. *God's Battle with the Monster. A Study in Biblical Imagery.* Leiden: Brill, 1973.

Waltke, B. K. *An Introduction to Biblical Hebrew Syntax.* Winona Lake, Ind.: Eisenbrauns, 1990.

Walton, J. H. "The Four Kingdoms in Daniel." *JETS* 29 (1986): 25–36.

Watts, R. E. "The Influence of the Isaianic New Exodus on the Gospel of Mark." Ph.D. diss., University of Cambridge, 1990.

Weber, O. *Ancient Judaism.* 1917–19. Reprint, Glencoe, Ill.: Free Press, 1952.

Weinfeld, M. "*kabod.*" In *Theologisches Handworterbuch zum Alten Testament (THWAT),* 4.23–40. Ed E. Jenni and C. Westermann. Zurich: Theologischer Verlag, 1971.

Weippert, M. "'Heiligerkrieg' in Israel und Assyrian." *ZAW* 84 (1972): 460–93.

Wellhausen, J. *Prolegomena to the History of Ancient Israel.* 1885.

_____. *Israelitische und judische Geschichte.* 3d ed. Berlin: Georg Reimer, 1897.

Wenham, D. *The Rediscovery of Jesus' Eschatological Discourse.* Sheffield: JSOT, 1984.

Wenham, G. *Genesis 1–15.* WBC, vol. 1. Waco, Tex.: Word, 1987.

Wild, R. A. "The Warrior and the Prisoner: Some Reflections on Ephesians 6:10–20." *CBQ* 46 (1984): 284–98.

Williamson, L. "Led in Triumph: Paul's Use of *Thriambeuo*," *Int* 22 (1968): 317–32.

Wink, W. *Naming the Powers*. Philadelphia: Fortress, 1984.

Witherington, B. *The Christology of Jesus*. Minneapolis: Fortress, 1990.

____. *Jesus, Paul and the End of the World*. Downers Grove, Ill.: Inter-Varsity Press, 1992

Woudstra, M. H. *The Ark of the Covenant from Conquest to Kingship*. Phillipsburg, N.J.: Presbyterian and Reformed, 1965.

Wright, N. T. *Colossians and Philemon*. TNTC. Grand Rapids: Eerdmans, 1986.

____. *The Climax of the Covenant*. Minneapolis: Fortress, 1991.

____. "Jerusalem in the New Testament." *Jerusalem Past and Present in the Purposes of God*, 53–77. Ed. P. W. L. Walker. Cambridge: Tyndale House, 1992.

Yadin, Y. *The Art of Warfare in Biblical Lands*. London: Weidenfeld and Nicolson, 1963.

Yates, R. "The Powers of Evil in the New Testament." *EQ* 52 (1980): 97–111.

____. "Colossians 2.15: Christ Triumphant." *NTS* 37 (1991): 573–91.

Yoder, J. *The Original Revolution: Essays on Christian Pacifism*. Scottdale, Pa.: Herald, 1977.

____. "'To Your Tents, O Israel': The Legacy of Israel's Experience with Holy War." *Studies in Religion/Sciences Religieuses* 18 (1989): 345–62.

◆ Subject Index ◆

◆ Author Index ◆

◆ Scripture and Other ◆ Literature Index